" All things are possible
to those who believe. "
              - Jesus Christ
                · Mark 9:23

THE MIND to *Heal*

Creating Health and Wellness in the Midst of Disease

Doreen Lecheler

WESTBOW
PRESS
A DIVISION OF THOMAS NELSON

Doreen Lecheler is a high performance consultant, speaker, author, and cancer-free coach. She is an affiliate of Excellent Cultures and the founder and president of VisionLinked, Inc.

Unless otherwise indicated, all Scripture quotations in this book are taken from the HOLY BIBLE, NEW INTERNATIONAL VERSION®. Copyright © 1973, 1978, 1984 by International Bible Society. Used by permission of Zondervan Publishing House. All rights reserved.

WestBow Press books may be ordered through booksellers or by contacting:

WestBow Press
A Division of Thomas Nelson
1663 Liberty Drive
Bloomington, IN 47403
www.westbowpress.com
1-(866) 928-1240

For a complete list of topics, materials, and programs by Doreen Lecheler send inquiries to: office@visionlinked.com
www.visionlinked.com

The Healed series:
Book One – The Spirit to Heal
Book Two – The Mind to Heal
Book Three – The Body to Heal

ISBN: 978-1-4497-5883-7 (sc)
ISBN: 978-1-4497-5882-0 (hc)
ISBN: 978-1-4497-5884-4 (e)

Library of Congress Control Number: 2012912228

Printed in the United States of America

WestBow Press rev. date: 09/04/2012

ACKNOWLEDGMENTS

THIS BOOK WOULD NOT BE possible except for the inspiration, living examples, and encouragement from the people God has purposed into my life. Those mentioned here and those who reside in my heart have all played a part in affirming my assignment to offer hope and healing in the midst of disease.

I first thank my husband, Brent, for his constant grace and sacrifice that have allowed me to explore possibilities and to grow in potential with ease, expectancy, and excitement. I hope you know the gift you are to me, and I thank you for this gift you've given me to pursue my destiny so freely.

I thank Lou and Diane Tice, founders of The Pacific Institute, for the work they've done around the world to help others think effectively, unleash potential, and grow in performance. As a twelve-year affiliate of the Institute, I had the privilege to learn and facilitate their curriculum within various organizations around the country. The opportunity they afforded me to become both a practitioner and consultant of this high-performance thinking gave me effective tools for a positive mind-set that would prove critical in my fight against "incurable" cancer.

I thank my friend Bruce Seidman, president of Sandler Training, for his avid support of my endeavors. Bruce is the poster boy for the enthusiasm of life! He has such a deep appreciation of the world around him and expresses heartfelt joy in the day-to-day things many of us overlook. Just thinking of Bruce makes me smile. Bruce, your support and our dialogue during my writing of this material sharpened my thinking and expression of what I wanted to say. Thank you for your investment of time in critiquing the content and distributing this information into a world that needs healing.

I've been so blessed by the inspiration and friendship of Cheryl Lehmann, founder of Victory Seekers. Cheryl's testimony of healing over many years and multiple diagnoses is worthy of a book itself. She personifies the principles and promises in this book and has compassionately poured out her life to help others overcome life-threatening disease. My love and admiration for Cheryl as an overcomer is only surpassed by my thrill and thankfulness that we are sisters together in the inheritance God so lavishly gives us.

Dedication

To Ray Weavill, Danette Schneider, and Robin Mammola, who have deeply touched my heart and played a precious role in who I am becoming. These friends live now in a higher glory as each has gone home to heaven over these past two years. They died far too young, but their faith, courage, and strength through the battle were an inspiration to all who knew them. You are each deeply missed, but I look forward to a heavenly reunion where "God will wipe away every tear from [our] eyes" (Revelation 7:17).

Contents

INTRODUCTION

IN BOOK ONE OF THE Healed series, *The Spirit to Heal* looks to our owner's manual, the Bible, to glean timeless truths around the topic of healing. What hopes and expectations can we hold of the One who created and knew us from the beginning? What elements were present in healing the sick and diseased that Jesus touched in each town and village He visited? The answers are central to how you see yourself and the circumstances you face.

Regardless of your religious views, there has not been a more profound and impacting healer in all of history than the person of Jesus Christ. His notoriety and following grew directly as a result of His compassion for people and His ability to heal their every disease and illness. Though it was His spiritual claims that ultimately had Him nailed to the cross, it was His healing ministry that drew Him out of obscurity and into a reverent following over three short years of public ministry. The miracles He did and those performed in His name give us insight into the power and authority He possessed, as well as our position and access through faith.

The Word of God found in Hebrew and New Testament Scripture gives us real substance in the things we hope for, including our healing. God's Word is so much more than positive thinking that easily disintegrates when the world doesn't deliver what we dream. God's Word powerfully and effectively gives us objective content upon which to set our thoughts and meditations. "I don't get well just because I *hope* so, I get well because God *says* so." The Scriptures deliver truth, assurance, peace, permission, and power as they instruct us on *what* to think. They are the foundation, or basis, for our hope of healing.

Book two of the Healed series, *The Mind to Heal*, focuses on our role and responsibility to receive healing. It provides cognitive tools and spiritual principles around *how* to think in the midst of disease. It takes us beyond the realm of passive hope to the reality of assertive faith. We don't merely hope, pray, and wait to see if we get well; we see ourselves well before there's any physical evidence of the kind. The way we think, the beliefs we hold, and the words we speak directly impact the results we see in our lives.

The principles, tools, and recommendations in this book are, in many cases, classic, high-performance, goal-setting essentials I have been delivering to organizations for many years. Proven, researched principles from the fields of cognitive psychology, emotional intelligence, and the burgeoning field of psychoneuroimmunology are just as efficacious for healing as they are for achieving bold organizational goals or outstanding personal performance. And their alignment with biblical precepts is amazingly on point.

In both instances, I felt so fortunate when I was delivered the news of my cancer diagnoses. As a consultant and practitioner of applied psychology and high-performance thinking, I was immediately aware of and attuned to the direction my thoughts were taking and how I was talking about my situation. Not only did I personally feel the benefits, but it was equally apparent to friends and family that I did not suffer anxiety, fear, worry, and hopelessness, which so often broadside us as we process such weighty news. Nor did I resign in defeat to my current reality with the attitude, "I guess it is what it is." I knew how to manage my mind so I didn't fall captive to the role of passive patient.

Several times, I found myself fending off anxiety-suppressing prescriptions the medical professionals pushed like candy. It wasn't some heroic stance or political platform I was trying to take. I simply didn't need them. Again and again, they would ask if I felt anxious and wanted something to "take the edge off."

"Well, I could be if I chose to," was my reply.

But that seemed like such a distraction and waste of time. I didn't need or desire that kind of personal drama and attention by telling everyone around me, as well as myself, that I was a "basket case." My focus was crystal-clear: on healing, on the end result I desired, and on where I wanted to go. And there was no anxiety, fear, or worry in that.

This information is not about denial of disease, wishful thinking, or "secret" solutions. Certainly the past forty years have produced numerous studies on how positive mental attitude directly impacts health and healing. Growing research on the mind-body connection has documented control groups of individuals in similar health conditions whose mind-sets about their health measurably impacted their healing, their physical abilities, and even their life spans.

Make no mistake ... managing your mind daily, controlling how you think, and being very intentional with your self-talk is serious business and requires attention and discipline, particularly when your physical symptoms and the doctor's prognosis appear contrary to what you desire. How do you handle disappointing or alarming news? How do you interact with well-wishers who mourn your condition? How do you control your mind-set in the midst of crisis? And what difference does it make?

If how we think, what we say, and what we do are not consistent with the hope of healing we desire, it becomes an upward battle of activity and a downward spiral of emotions as we consciously are dying to live but subconsciously living to die.

There is a better, more effective way.

This book gives you tools and principles to take control. I pray you make that healing choice.

Doreen Lecheler

Picture Perfect:
Creating Health and Wellness
in the Midst of Disease

Blog entry: April 24, 2009

Purpose

WELL I DEFINITELY DIDN'T EXPECT to find myself here, starting a weekly blog … at least not about myself. Being the psychologizing, socio-theological magnet that I am, you would more usually find me writing about building peak performance, transforming individual and collective behavior, or creating purpose-filled, sustainable change. I suppose in a very real and vulnerable way, I'll still be doing that. It's just now the principles and processes will be clothed in the real-life drama of my own journey.

I must first start by emphasizing it is not my intent to paint a broad brushstroke around disease, healing, and wholeness when the nuances of each person's experience are so vast and personal. More nearly, this is my personal story—physical, emotional, and spiritual—and the journey of a tremendous opportunity to experience and share how I'm living through and by everything I profess to believe. It kind of makes me wonder if perhaps I wasn't made exactly for this time and challenge. But that's a whole different blog entry for a whole other day.

As many of you already know, I've spent the past two months undergoing a battery of tests that report a recurrence of breast cancer advanced to stage four and metastasized to the spine. It's been quite a shocker for me actually. I'm healthy. I feel great. I exercise daily, there's no stress in my life, and I'm eating pure, whole foods (no sugar, no flour!). On top of that, my surgeon in 2006 declared my first diagnosis as a contained, "garden-variety," stage one breast cancer. The sentinel nodes were clean; therefore, a simple lumpectomy, thirty-three days of radiation, and a daily pill were sufficient. It was a blip on my radar screen—removed and gone— and life moved on.

Okay, maybe it wasn't as uneventful as all that. There were some very important and significant life lessons learned. Pitfalls I stumbled right into. Ones I should have known better given my profession, training, and background. Ones that conflicted with everything I know about how the mind works and how what we think and what we say have a direct impact on the results in our lives.

Determined to do it better the next time, I'm using "Picture Perfect" as a personal diary to keep the current reality dialogue to a minimum (please know how very much I cherish your love and prayers and support, but the repetition of updates can get so very weary), as well as a teaching tool to reinforce for myself and share with others truths to empower us to co-create our own wellness in the midst of disease.

So, I leave next week with my mother for a consultation at Memorial Sloan Kettering in NYC. The love, support, and advocacy of friends like Micki Molonari and Tania Anderson got me a highly coveted slot on Dr. Traina's calendar before she starts her daily medical routine. I'm anxious to hear what's available or cutting-edge or even on the clinical trial list for me. At the end of next week, I'm scheduled for surgery at Saint Joseph's Cancer Center in Towson, Maryland, to have cancerous lymph nodes removed.

In the meantime, while I've still got my digging arm, I've got a date this weekend with 120 sun-loving tulip bulbs and a wanting garden. I picture only beautiful things growing this summer.

Healing hugs,
Doreen

Choose Life:
Laying the Foundation for Hope and Healing

"THIS DAY I CALL HEAVEN and earth as witnesses against you that I have set before you life and death, blessings and curses. Now choose life, so that you and your children may live" (Deuteronomy 30:19).

Having just undergone tests, you are sitting in front of a doctor who hands you a bombshell.

"I'm sorry, but you have cancer."

Your body sits numb and motionless as an explosion of thoughts racks your mind. The fear and weightiness of this new reality is almost too surreal to grasp. "Cancer! Why me? What happens next?"

The days and weeks that follow are an agonizing unknown as you migrate from one test to another to determine the depth and breadth of the disease inhabiting your body. A tsunami of information –medical facts and figures, terms and procedures, input from multiple sources, options, and emotions—crashes upon you.

With so many decisions to make, steps to take, and directions to go, it is easy to get swept up in the flurry of activity orchestrated around you from the medical professionals in the know. And though science has yet to determine why some bodies effectively fight off abnormal cells while others don't, and though cancer rates continue to grow at an alarming rate, and though medicine is still a long way from curing the disease, we tend to defer our futures and our fates to the medical experts who practice at this growing pandemic called cancer.

A West Point commandeer once said, "When face-to-face with the enemy on the battlefield, I've yet to see a man not turn to God in his time of need." The same could be true of this battle. A glimpse of mortality can cause even the most hard-hearted and self-sufficient to raise his hands to God in hope of being miraculously rescued from impending doom. We instinctively seek to avoid pain. We secretly pray for miracles, and miracles do happen.

For others, the road to wellness takes a different route. It's much more than that miraculous moment when the descending hand of God touches us with mercy and power. Instead, healing is a process, a journey, an adventure. We co-labor with God toward our destination down a path fraught with choices to make, mountains to climb, and pitfalls to avoid. It is a faith-filled opportunity to grasp the ascending hand of God and live above our circumstances rather than in the thick of them.

But the choices we make or don't make along the way carry physical, spiritual, and psychological consequences, and knowing this vastly impacts our ability to create health and wellness in the midst of disease.

Among these myriad of choices, the most important is often overlooked yet sets the course for the journey we undertake: "Do I live or die?" Do I choose life, healing, and wholeness? Or do I choose death, disease, and sickness?

To some, those questions may appear arrogantly abrasive, ridiculously self-evident, or startlingly presumptuous. Doesn't everyone desire to get well? Don't we all choose life? Do we even get to choose at all?

Since the foundation of humankind, we have been endowed with free will—the ability to choose. In the cosmic creation of man, the God of the universe, who desires personal intimacy with each one of us, understood true relationships are fostered in freedom not force. And though there is that spirit place within us, our connection to the Divine is not automatic. Though we are all God's creation, we are not all His children. Though made in His image, God's Spirit is not within us unless we consciously choose. He stands at the doors of our hearts and knocks. We decide whether to let Him in. That's how we were created; that's how we're wired. It's a powerful and mysterious paradox: though completely sovereign, God is the consummate gentleman who never thrusts Himself upon us. Yes, choice always carries the risk of refusal and rejection. We are self-determined individuals who decide what fills our spirit-void, what or whom we will serve, and the extent to which we will serve it. And we all serve something—either by intent or neglect.

Our lives are the proverbial fork in the road where we are constantly confronted with momentary decisions about options, actions, and perspectives we will take. Essential to this idea is that choices have consequences. While we have the fundamental right to choose, we also need to accept that we are fully accountable for the results of those choices rather than maintaining the notion of entitlement that has become so popular in our modern culture.

Choosing life is a God-ordained privilege, but it also needs to be a deliberate, conscious, and consistent act on our part. Life becomes the filter through which we make our healing choices.

Am I talking about my illness or my vision of health?

Are my thoughts and attitudes consistent with my goal of healing?

Is what I'm feeding my body—physically, emotionally, and spiritually—allowing wellness to take root in me?

We are whole people—spirit, mind, and body. Most of us live fairly dissected lives, which only compromises our strength and defenses. Therefore, if it is health and healing we desire, we must develop a comprehensive, integrated strategy to address the root causes of illness in our lives. Our beliefs, thoughts, words, and actions must be aligned, intentional, and designed to promote health if we hope to receive and nurture the reality of healing within us.

Choosing life has its very foundations rooted in God. It's not about avoiding the sting of death but about embracing the perspective, promises, and power available to us as children of the Almighty. [If that currently is not your worldview or if you need more support to understand your position in God, please refer to The Spirit to Heal, at www.TheSpiritToHeal.com]

Choosing life is not merely positive wishful thinking; it is a very real option God lavishes upon us. It is an outrageous opportunity to step into a supernatural realm of relationship, trust, peace, and thankfulness while chaos outwardly tries to consume us.

I admit I didn't always feel that way. Yes, I understood we live in a fallen world. Bad things happen to "good" people all the time. Genetics, aging, lifestyle choices, past conditioning, and environmental factors all impact our longevity, immune system, and ability to fight disease. But my religious conditioning over the years informed me that because God is sovereign, all things come from Him, good and bad—even disease. If I have it and He doesn't heal it, I'm resigned to a guessing game of trying to discover one or all of the following:

Am I not doing something right?

Am I being punished?

Does God want to shape up my character or build up my faith?

Is He trying to draw me closer to Him?

Do I deserve healing?

Has He got something better for me (heaven)?

Does God intervene in this day and age?

Meting out pain and affliction to His covenant, faith-filled children just to get our attention (which I thought He already had) seemed diametrically opposed to the idea of the God of love and reconciliation. That concept cloaked in "mystery" was a hard pill to swallow. In fact, I couldn't; it got stuck in my throat every time. I began to search the Word of God to clarify His character and my responsibility as I journeyed through my own diagnosis of stage four cancer with metastases to the bone.

When I received news of how the nonaggressive, stage-one cancer that had been effectively treated in 2006 had now advanced to stage four and was growing on my spine, I naturally assumed it was the will of God. The odds of such a recurrence based on my original diagnosis were less than 1 percent. Such an oddity must have had some divine origin and purpose. Otherwise, none of it made sense. I was doing everything "right" to care for my body on a physical, psychological, and spiritual level, or so I thought. I began a deep and intense search to understand how to effectively live out my days. I was determined to gracefully accept whatever came my way. But very different mindsets and activities are required for either accepting death or preparing for battle. I was prepared to make the most of either one—I just needed to understand what course I should take so I wouldn't waste precious time or miss important opportunities. It was in this search for meaning and direction that I found hope, permission, and power to choose life (see The Spirit to Heal).

Choosing life is an attitude, a perspective, a way of thinking, and a way of living. Choosing life says, "Cancer may be here, but it doesn't have the right to stay here." It acknowledges the doctors' diagnoses as the physical, medical reality of the world they live in each day without accepting that reality as yours. Choosing life takes on a warrior spirit that says "I know who I am and to Whom I belong; I know my rights and privileges as a child of the Most High; and I fight from a position of authority and victory, not from a position of fear, doubt, and defeat." Choosing life differentiates the inevitability of death we all face one day from allowing disease to ravage, steal, and destroy us. "I know I have to die someday, but it won't be from cancer." This is the battle cry of the believer.

My husband is brilliant for coming up with profound statements of the obvious. We call them "Brent-isms." One of my favorite goes like this, "If you live long enough, you'll eventually die." It's true.

We're all marked with an expiration date. Quite honestly, I am not interested in achieving some centenarian goal if it means I've watched my loved ones all die before me and my body no longer has the capacity to serve, teach, and encourage others. Right or wrong, I'm just being honest. I have no fear of death or desire to live forever on this side of life. I have such a longing for heaven and a vision for living in the Son that the ancient writings of the Jewish scholar, Pharisee, and eventual apostle, Paul of Tarsus, resonate in my heart, "For me to live is Christ and to die is gain" (Philippians 1:21).

But a critical element to our understanding of healing is that to *not* consciously choose is still a choice. It's not enough to remain ambivalent or indecisive. You cannot simply play the role of passenger on your road to recovery. You need to have a target, a goal, an objective. If you aim at nothing, you will hit it every time. The same is true when there are too many choices. If we aim at everything, we wind up hitting nothing. You may instinctively "hope" to be healed, but unless life and healing become vivid end results, even in spite of the medical "reality" around you, you unknowingly, unconsciously sabotage the very environment of healing you require. You must make life, healing, and wholeness your conscious and subconscious end result, no matter the circumstances surrounding you.

Being a person active in a community of faith, I have witnessed so many devoted, well-meaning Christians make the mistake of being confused or careless about their situation. They certainly hope and pray for healing but relinquish their own responsibility. It seems as though it's an all-or-nothing proposition as they falter over the sovereignty of God and their freedom to choose life or death.

In that sentiment, it is also important to recognize not everyone will choose life. For better or worse, we cannot impose our will to fight on others. We can hope, pray, encourage, and model the choice to fight for life, but we must also allow others the freedom to say no or "Enough" without guilt or condemnation.

Over the past two years, I have witnessed one too many scenarios where doctors, in their limited ability to arrest an advancing disease, pronounced a death sentence. In several of these incidences, precious patients acknowledged and sanctioned the prescribed timeline for their end of life. Without realizing it, they subconsciously adopted someone else's opinion as their reality. In one extreme case of stage four pancreatic cancer, the woman was recommended to go to hospice where she would have three to four months to live. Her family moved her in on Friday. She was dead on Tuesday. She was not interested in or convinced of continuing in the fight if death was the inevitable goal at the end of 160 days. For her, it was over. She gave up her will and spirit to live. Her choice was to leave the physical realm of life as we know it.

But even in the moment where you no longer choose life, my hope and prayer for you is twofold. First, I pray you allow that choice to belong to you—not the "experts" in their field. Second, I pray your choice is motivated and empowered by an intentional, Spirit-filled running toward heaven rather than a hopeless, poverty-stricken limping toward defeat.

Until the moment of our last earthly breath, may we choose life and love others with reckless abundance —without reservation, regret, or retreat.

Picture Perfect:
Creating Health and Wellness
in the Midst of Disease

Blog entry: May 8, 2009

Into View

I T WAS A WHIRLWIND LAST week—so much so I couldn't tell whether I was riding home on the Amtrak train or being run over by it. I was so physically exhausted I hurt.

I don't know why I was so shot. My mom and I love NYC, and we had a really nice time together. I was so looking forward to spending a couple of days alone with her. And she desperately needed to feel informed and part of the process.

We left early on Monday morning and met my Aunt Joanie and Cousin Brian for lunch at a yummy Thai restaurant in the East Village. We did some much-needed retail therapy at Bloomingdales—mostly because it was around the corner from our European-populated "boutique" hotel. We indulged on a delicious Mediterranean dinner and got an early bedtime in order to be ready for our 7:30 a.m. appointment at Sloan-Kettering.

Drs. Traina and Dang are beautiful, sensitive, intelligent women who were quite generous with their time. We left armed with information, options, and a glimmer of hope. The doctors felt that without a bone biopsy on my spine, they could not conclusively say it was incurable cancer. I immediately called my surgeon and pleaded with his office to find me a slot during Friday's surgery schedule to have a biopsy performed. I figured if I was going to feel like bunk, why not go for the gusto and do it all at once.

I tried to be levelheaded and even-handed, but I must confess I saw this as a wonderful opportunity for God to shine and manifest in my body what I already knew in my head and heart to be true, that "by his stripes I am [already] healed" (Isaiah 53:5; emphasis, mine). Wouldn't that be a marvelous miracle? And as for my friends and family who live more by what can be seen rather than by faith—the substance of things hoped for—they could chalk it up to a case of misdiagnosis. All the same, I would be looking at four to six months of chemo and a daily pill. I could certainly live with that.

While recuperating on the couch this weekend, I rented Slumdog Millionaire, a heart-wrenching but marvelously done film that starkly reinforced to me the wonder and blessing it is that I happened to be born and raised in the abundance of the United States. Having firsthand experience of third-world medicine through my previous work with Project C.U.R.E., I couldn't help but thank God for world-class hospitals and state-of-the-art equipment, insurance, anesthesia, and that wonderful drug they give you to make you forget the entire day's events!

By Tuesday morning, I was wondering why I hadn't heard from the surgeon about the bone biopsy results on my spine. I typed out my e-mail to him (he's one of those 24/7 Blackberry guys who is always available and quick to respond). With the mixed emotions of eagerness and hesitancy you feel before dropping your very last coin into a slot machine, I pressed the SEND button and focused on preparing for the seven executive coaching calls I had to complete for a new client project while I waited.

Within fifteen minutes, Dr. Schultz replied. Good news—they had removed and tested nineteen lymph nodes that drain the breast, and only one—the original one—tested positive for cancer. Bad news—the bone biopsy confirmed metastases on the spine. Conclusively, I was diagnosed with stage four, incurable cancer.

I think my stomach secreted a gallon of acid because I felt suddenly sick. Then sad. Then angry. I had my little "boo hoo" fest in between trying to fold laundry and then thanked God there were seven conference calls waiting to compete for my energy and focus. Oh, for those tender mercies and little blessings that come to us in disguise. They allowed me to blink away the blur of these past nine days, refocus, and let the real picture of who I am and what I'm called to do come into view. It was a gift, a productive and purpose-filled day. And that's the picture I hold to.

Healing hugs,
Doreen

Choose Alignment:
Developing a Strategic Defense

"FINALLY, BE STRONG IN THE Lord and in his mighty power. Put on the full armor of God so that you can take your stand" (Ephesians 6:10–11).

September 11, 2001 took on a much greater significance for me than simply celebrating my mother's birthday, as it became an American national calamity of global proportions for all peace-abiding, democracy-loving peoples of the world. The invasion into our national security and our hearts was shocking and cataclysmic.

As a nation, we didn't see it coming. We were totally unprepared and unsuspecting of this unprecedented occurrence on mainland soil. With our defenses down, we were left scrambling for information, tactics, and emotional support.

Military experts defined the perpetrators as a new kind of enemy. Traditional, historic warfare was no longer in play. The enemy's tactics were stealth, deceptive and devastating. Our armed forces surmised this was a whole new battlefield that required breakthrough thinking.

This terrorizing assault thrust us into an innovative strategy— the formation of Homeland Security. Intelligence and protective agencies like the CIA, FBI, National Guard, Port Authority, and others, who historically had been independent and withholding from one another, now had to cooperate, collaborate, and communicate with a common language to share information, work together, and bring security back to our nation. It would require nothing less than a comprehensive, master strategy among these previously autonomous groups. The organization I was affiliated with, The Pacific Institute, was contracted to help build that culture of cohesion.

The diagnosis of chronic disease is, in many ways, like experiencing your own 9/11 moment. It is an unparalleled event where you've just discovered your own enemy invasion.

For people who see themselves as unhealthy or who have been battling very real and evident symptoms, the medical news usually confirms or matches the picture they already hold in their minds about who they are: "Something is wrong with me. I am sick."

And for others who see themselves as relatively healthy and fit, the news can create tremendous tension: "How can this be? I'm a healthy person. I'm too young for this!" The pictures don't match.

How we see ourselves in the midst of disease is foundational to whether we will actively pursue and expect healing or whether we will resign and passively hope healing might come our way. One is an ardent advocate; the other a passive patient. The desire is the same ... healing. But one will pursue it with positive assurance; the other will cross their fingers with cautious optimism.

The response to my first diagnosis in 2006 was utter shock. You see, I didn't see myself as a sick person. I was health-conscious, fit, and athletic. I always had been. I was forty-five years young with a five-year old son who would be starting kindergarten in three weeks. I had no symptoms that would make me suspect. In my mind, cancer was for sick people, old people, people genetically predisposed, or people who just didn't bother to properly take care of themselves. The idea of personally having cancer was far too foreign from my picture of health. It made the chasm particularly deep for me and the fall especially treacherous.

What about you? Are you a healthy person battling a disease that shouldn't be there? Or are you a sick person who seems to have one issue after the next? Are you worthy of being healed? Or is it impossible or too late in your mind? Is it God's will for you to be healed?

The image you hold of yourself has everything to do with the level of energy, motivation, drive, tenacity, resiliency, and commitment necessary for the healing process. It requires constant monitoring of your thoughts, words, and actions, particularly when you are in the thick of tests, diagnoses, treatments, and doctor visits. It can be extremely challenging to think and talk about circumstances when doctors are saying one thing and we are goal-setting for another. From my two experiences with breast cancer, I often commented, "Cancer is more a battle of the mind than it is of the body." My body has already been given all it needs to restore itself; it's my mind and emotions that doubt, question, and compromise my health and wholeness at any moment in life. Healing has its best advantage when what we want, what we do, and how we see ourselves are in steadfast alignment.

Just as the Department of Defense wouldn't think of going into war without employing the full military resources of air, land, and sea, your personal battle can be no different. You must engage and align your spirit, mind, and body, pulling together all the strength of the resources available to you for this fight.

Alignment is more than just our best defense. It is an offensive strike where we properly place our spirit in connection with the Divine in order to receive in our minds and bodies all we need for life and godliness (2 Peter 1:3–4). The most comprehensive, all-out affront on the enemy invasion within you is to bring your body, your mind, and your spirit into alignment with the person you were created in potential to be. Through conscious commitment, you must begin to examine and assess your combat strength in each of these three areas. To disregard one as insignificant or irrelevant is like going on an enemy attack and telling your airmen you don't need them. Combat military would never think of sending in ground and sea forces without the surveillance, perspective, and advantage from the air. Nor would they commission troops who are not adequately armed with the basic training to fight the battle.

Too often, we live dissected lives and disregard the health and wellness that are by-products of living in holistic alignment. Certainly there are environmental and genetic factors contributing to disease, but our years of physical, psychological, and/or spiritual neglect and imbalance have a direct impact on our ability to either host or combat the enemy invasion of disease.

When I am hired to build high-performing cultures in all types of organizations, a common plight I diagnose is where various departments operate independently of one another. It's called having organizational "silos" where perhaps the sales and marketing department may be at odds with customer service that is also disconnected from manufacturing. These splinters or factions within the same organization cause it to break down and dysfunction. Their misguided thinking, behaviors, and processes lose sight of the overall vision and purpose of the organization. Instead, their tunnel vision is limited to departmental desires and objectives at the expense of the whole. As a result, turf wars cause internal competition with one another rather than using their assigned assets to rally against competitors invading their marketplace. Communication is often poor, negative, and accusatory. The internal fighting causes reactive tendencies, withholding of valuable information, and loss of synergies. The outcomes are inefficient uses of resources, redundancies in the organization, taxing bureaucratic overhead, and a toxic, defensive culture.

While individuals are not organizations, we are organisms who function in much the same way. We are body, mind, and spirit, meant to operate in relation to each other. The body experiences the natural realm through sensory perception, and its outcomes physically manifest and are measured by our *Performance*. The mind processes information, stores beliefs, and reinforces our perspectives, which affect the release of our *Potential*. And the spirit shapes our worldview, arouses motivations, and reveals intent. It is the seat of vision, the fuel for values, and the fount of *Purpose*.

When our Purpose (spirit), Potential (mind), and Performance (body) are in alignment, we are at our most whole, productive, and healthy self. When we dissect, or silo, our lives, we, like organizations, become inefficient, less effective, and innately vulnerable to dis-ease in our lives and our bodies. To the extent we are out of balance or out of order, we weaken our defenses and are in danger of attack.

One reason we build a segmented understanding of ourselves is because the mind tends to makes sense of the world by labeling or compartmentalizing things. Therefore, we tend to see the body, mind, and spirit as distinct entities pictured in the following manner:

Body　　Mind　　Spirit

Such a view can lead to the erroneous thinking that our emphasis placed in one area doesn't impact or distract from the others. But you remain at a weakened disadvantage if you focus on things of a spiritual nature yet disregard what you put in your mouth or the thoughts you feed your mind. Likewise, you can fixate on eating only pure, whole foods and have a disciplined exercise regime, but if your spirit is selfish or your thoughts are plagued with bitterness, fear, and strife, your body alone will offer little vaccination for your plight. Like most things in life, balance is key, but balance requires intention and attention. It does not happen by neglect.

In truth, a more accurate depiction of the interdependence and effect each facet of our being has on the other is to see our spirit, mind, and body as a cord of three strands not easily broken (Ecclesiastes 4:12).

The unraveling or weakening of one compromises the strength of the whole. And yet it is possible to give yourself wholly to the wrong things. Developing a strategic defense against disease requires attention to balance but also to the priority of putting first things first. You must align your spirit first to be consistent with the promise of abundant life as Jesus described in John 10:10. Why? Because your spirit is the seat of your worldview, vision, and values. It's from your spirit that you feed your mind. The mind and body always follow.

Our modern Western culture idolizes an inverted model of self-love and self-sufficiency first as the apex for living. We begin with ourselves (body) because, indeed, "we are entitled to it." And our thinking adjusts to support the lifestyle we desire. The problem with that inverted and perverted thinking is that when we are entirely self-focused first, enough is never enough. There is an insatiable need for more that does not satisfy our deepest, spirit-driven longings. And we eventually become the slave to our own indulgences, unable to control our cravings, emotions, and impulses. As long as we try to fulfill the eternal things of the spirit—ultimate peace, joy, truth, happiness, and love—with the temporary things of this natural, decaying world, we will always come up short. Abundant life comes when we allow the Spirit of creation to take hold of our spirit in order to transform our thinking and produce outcomes where we live authentically from ourselves and toward others here on Earth as it is in heaven.

As we adopt the proper alignment of spirit, mind, and body, we begin to see the challenges we face as mere symptoms of much larger and deeper root causes. The real danger of an iceberg is not what we see or experience on the surface but what lies below. To avoid the peril of certain death, it requires a change of perspective to see all there is to see.

Picture Perfect:
Creating Health and Wellness
in the Midst of Disease

Blog Entry: May 15, 2009

Picture of Hope

I DON'T DO WELL WITH LIMITATIONS. In fact, one sure-fire way to get me going is to tell me there's no way to accomplish what I've set out to do. As far as I can remember, I've always been this way. Nature or nurture? Who knows? But I don't like anything or anyone trying to keep me down (and I wonder where Nicholas gets his contrarian personality???). And so this past week has been a bit of a challenge for me.

Because they removed nineteen lymph nodes under my right arm, a Jackson Pratt drainage device was stitched into me to aid the healing process. Gauze and tape—not to be removed or dampened—disguise the origin of the plastic tube. But I can only imagine the source is stitched somewhere into my incision. Twice daily, Brent drains, measures, and notes the fluid levels collecting at the bottom in a suction cup the size of a baseball. Why the tube needs to extend the length of my torso down to my kneecaps escapes me. And though I have a large pin to gather and attach it to the waistband of my clothes, the bulbous contraption and transparent coil of tubing create a fashion challenge for keeping my fluids discreetly out of public view. Needless to say, I haven't gone out much.

I was hoping to have this nuisance removed this past Monday. Dr. Schultz said I could expect about ten days. Well ten days have come and gone, and my levels are not diminishing. They started to, but then I got somewhat active again—trying to wash and style my own hair, iron Nic's school clothes, and not ask for help every time I needed something moved, put away, or opened. Hand in hand with my aversion to limitations is my apparent inability to ask for and receive help. Resolved that self-reliance and pride lost out this week, and I would be wearing my alien attachment to Rehoboth Beach for a family weekend away, I was stunned to get the coveted call. The tube comes out today. I get to throw self-consciousness to the wind and pack my typical beach garb. Hope wins!

But not so much so last Thursday with my trip to Johns Hopkins. This was my second consultation with yet another esteemed oncologist at yet another prestigious cancer center. This time, Brent and my mom joined me for a quick day trip outside of Baltimore.

It started out well. The doctor seemed interested, informed, and caring. Then I noted the pause of his pen and the arch of his brow when I responded to his question about how I felt. Perhaps he's just accustomed to the fear and hopelessness surrounding patients with cancer metastases. Perhaps he didn't care for my brand of faith and positive mental attitude. But when I told him I felt blessed, he looked at me as if I just had a frontal lobotomy. His expression prompted elaboration on my part as I tried to explain the overwhelming love, support, and tenderness I have experienced from God, family, and friends. Quite frankly, I'm not sure he bought it. He countered with his own dose of reality by offering statistics far from what we imagined or hoped for. When Brent tried to share an antidote given by my surgeon about his mother's cancer and the eighteen-year tenure she lived given the level of pervasiveness, the doctor dismissed our expectations by telling us it was "a nice story." He prided himself and his practice on conservatism and told us they don't like to raise hopes and disappoint people. I was screaming inside, "What the heck's the difference?" What's wrong with hope? Why not picture the possibilities, expect miracles, die to live rather than live to die? It was all I could do to not hurl my business card into his lap and recount studies on the impact of faith, belief, and healing. It took the rest of the evening and the following day to shake off his dismal view. It was my choice—either accept his picture and live in despair or believe God and choose abundant life. He'll see ... I'm anything but a statistic.

Healing hugs,
Doreen

Choose Truth:
Harnessing the Power of Perspective

One day, the father of a very wealthy family took his son on a trip to the country with the express purpose of showing him how poor people live. They spent a couple of days and nights on the farm of what would be considered a very poor family. On their return from their trip, the father asked his son, "How was the trip?"

"It was great, Dad."

"Did you see how poor people live?" The father asked.

"Oh, yeah," said the son.

"So, tell me. What did you learn from the trip?" asked the father.

The son answered, "I saw that we have one dog, and they had four. We have a pool that reaches to the middle of our garden, and they have a creek that has no end. We have imported lanterns in our garden, and they have the stars at night. Our patio reaches to the front yard, and they have the whole horizon. We have a small piece of land to live on, and they have fields that go beyond our sight. We have servants who serve us, but they serve others. We buy our food, but they grow theirs. We have

walls around our property to protect us; they have
friends to protect them."
The boy's father was speechless.
Then his son added, "Thanks, Dad, for showing me
how poor we are."

Unknown

Y OUR ABILITY TO EARNESTLY CHOOSE life and effectively abide
in a healing environment has everything to do with how you
think. The danger for us all is we rarely take time to reflect on what
we think about. Our beliefs, habits, expectations, and responses are
automatic, subconsciously programmed thoughts and attitudes—
unless, of course, we understand how the mind works. In other
words, we know *how* to think.

Having a proper perspective is not about soft, mushy sentiment
or plastic smiles plastered across fearful faces. There is real power
in perspective. And though it has been the basis of my work for
creating high-performance individuals and organizational cultures,
it has never been more critical than when helping others as well
as myself overcome disease. Why? Because it has everything to
do with who you'll put in control of your life; what information
you'll hear and stand upon; what choices are available to you; and
what opportunities you'll pursue. It impacts your emotions and
even your physiology—where worry, stress, and fear feed an already
compromised immune system. It builds, sustains, or destroys energy,
resiliency, and hope. It's the difference between a warrior spirit and
a passive patient.

Scientific research over the past sixty-plus years into how we
think and how the mind works shows there is a direct correlation
between our perspective and the quality of our life. Biblically, it
is depicted, "For as a man thinks in his heart, so is he" (Proverbs
23:7). Where you are right now in any area of your life—financially,
relationally, spiritually, physically, emotionally—is the result of your
perspective or best thinking at this moment. And though you may

consciously have the strongest motivation and desire for healing, if your subconscious thoughts, habits, attitudes, and expectations are not aligned with your goal, you will effectively sabotage the very thing you hope for—life and wholeness.

As a Man Thinks in His Heart …

The word *perspective* has its roots in the Latin *perspectivus*, meaning, "sight, optical," and in the French *perspicere*, meaning to look through or see clearly. In modern cognitive terms, perspective is more nearly how we see things. It's our point of view; what we often label our truth or reality.

How we look at things makes a difference. We know that by now—at least, intellectually speaking. We've read it, we've heard it, and we may have even put it into practice in particular areas of our lives. It is the topic of most inspirational life and business success principles. Change the way you think and you begin to change the way your life goes.

How? I call it the Pebble Effect. Drop a stone into the water, and its impact is not stagnant or insignificant. Though with the naked eye it may appear to simply sink to the bottom, below the water's surface, disruption of the "normal" produces great energy, creating a rippling effect whose circumference spreads far and wide.

This notion was first popularized in 1963 when Edward Lorenz published a paper on his theory of the "Butterfly Effect." A butterfly flapping its wings can cause enough growing energy to cause a tornado in a different location clear across the world. Based on Chaos Theory and the Law of Sensitive Dependence, cause effects consequences far beyond the original boundaries.

The same is true of our beliefs and words. Our contemporary Western culture has so twisted the true idea of freedom—liberation from bondage or slavery to someone or something—into entitlement—I am my own person, and I have the right to do or say or think whatever I want as long as I don't "harm" anyone else. The problem with that thinking is that while we *are* self-determined—meaning, we make our own choices—we are *not* self-sufficient. Our choices aren't independent, isolated occurrences; their rippling effect always impacts others as well as other areas of our own lives. The beliefs we voice and enact have the replicating power to effect change physically, emotionally, and spiritually in ourselves and in our world.

If we truly understood this concept, we would see we are far too careless about what we say and do. That's why God, through His Word, implores us to be transformed by the renewing of our mind (Romans 12:2), to guard our thoughts and hold them captive (2 Corinthians 10:5), and to watch the very words we utter from our lips (Proverbs 18:21). Among the limitless attributes of our Creator God, He is the original and ultimate psychologist (aka, "Wonderful Counselor"). Through the ancient biblical writers, God inspired over fourteen hundred verses about the mind, our thinking, knowledge, wisdom, and understanding, as well as hundreds of verses emphasizing the critical nature of how and what we speak.

Did He proclaim these things just to restrict our freedom? No, quite the opposite! He knew that stamped in His image, our words and perspectives have power—the power to create life or death. Our beliefs and words create energy that has consequences, not only for us but also for others and even generations to come. Perspective either frees us or binds us. It expands us or limits us. It heals us or harms us. It determines the depth and breadth and the quality and quantity of the opportunities we'll see, information we'll receive, and choices we'll make.

Art Lindsley, senior fellow at the C. S. Lewis Institute, used agrarian concepts of sowing and reaping to effectively illustrate the far-reaching impact of perspective:

> Sow a thought; reap an act.
> Sow an act; reap a habit.

Sow a habit; reap a lifestyle.

Sow a lifestyle; reap a destiny.

So how do we dig ourselves out of circumstances we have sown that stifle life so we can create a destiny of hope, health, and wholeness? Albert Einstein penned, "No problem can be solved on the same level [of thinking] that it was created." We need an upgrade in our current level of thinking.

An effective goal of healing, as with any goal we set in life, involves a seven-step process that includes *Realization, Reflection, Revelation, Release, Realignment, Restoration,* and *Rejoicing. Realization* begins with the acknowledgment of the need and desire for change, the recognition and confession that it's time to do things differently. It's a spirit declaration that we are living far below the potential God has purposed for us physically, spiritually, and/or psychologically. *Realization* is the initial motivation to pursue new outcomes for our lives.

The next step to your wellness is awareness—conscious awareness—of your subconscious thinking patterns through the process of self-*reflection.* You need to become cognizant of how you think, what you're dwelling upon, and how you're speaking about your situation to yourself and to others. All the self-help materials in the world and all the physical endeavors you pursue will be to little avail if you don't hold within you the proper perspective of positive expectancy. You must control the way you think.

Quiet, thoughtful *reflection* is designed to lead you to *revelation*—"So *that's* what's holding me back!" *Revelation* delves deeper than our surface-level symptoms to unearth the root of wrong thinking and limiting attitudes that block our potential for wholeness. *Revelation* exposes the core cause for change and opportunity to *release* the emotional attachments that created such subconscious strongholds in the first place. *Reflection* for *revelation* is the beginning of the seven-step process I will unfold further, but it is the foundation for all constructive goal achievement, which includes your health.

Reflection Activity

As powerful as this information is, this book will offer little help to you if you simply read it for new content. Information without encounter leads to expanded knowledge not transformational change or healing. How many times have you heard an inspirational message or profound wisdom that impacted you for the moment but caused no sustainable change in your life? How many times have you intellectually agreed with a new idea, the truth may even have pierced through to your heart, but you walked away the same person? If you're like most of us, the answer is "one too many." That's because growth, development, and change require engagement. You cannot be a passive learner.

So grab a pen, and begin a new journal. Take a few moments to thoughtfully respond to the Reflection Activities throughout this book. Come back to these questions on a regular basis, as they will form the habit of reflection and revelation that are essential to your healing.

1. What seeds am I currently sowing into my circumstances? Fear? Resignation? Anger? Anxiety? Chaos? Depression? Worry? Optimism? Hope? Peace?

2. As I think about my body, the doctor's prognosis, and the way I'm talking about my situation, what are my most dominant emotions, beliefs, habits, and expectations?

3. Write out the following column headings: My Health, My Prognosis, My Doctors, My Future. Below each heading, list the words, adjectives, and phrases that quickly come to mind. Don't analyze each thought before writing. Don't try to be "correct." Simply write down everything as it surfaces. Be as exhaustive in your responses as possible.

4. In what areas above are my perspectives choosing life? What areas are working against my desire to choose life?

5. Which ones do I want to change, and what would that look like? Write it out, and be specific.

Taking Control

The quality of information you hold in your mind has a direct impact on your quality of life. It begins with how you receive and respond to information about the world around you and is formulated by the subconscious question that directs your destiny, "Who is in control?"

Many individuals attribute their lack of success, significance, or satisfaction to situations or circumstances outside themselves. The economy, the boss, company policies, the kids, their upbringing, their health, their schedules, the "experts," etc. all determine what opportunities are available to them. They place control of and blame for their lives on people and situations outside themselves. It is known as having an external locus of control where we place the accountability and responsibility for our own lives on someone else's shoulders.

We know from living life there are circumstances and occasions that can hit us hard and unsuspecting, where we are totally out of our control. Bad things do happen to good people all the time. And while we may not have knowingly created the circumstances, we can choose how we will respond, what we will believe, what we will say, and how we will say it. It feels uncomfortable and perhaps a bit unfair, but pain is part of learning who we really are. I didn't always feel that way. And I certainly didn't make healthy choices as a young girl growing up with hurts and disappointments in my life.

At age nine, I left the fun and familiar safety net of my large, closely connected, extended family. My parents moved us seven hours away to Harrisburg, Pennsylvania, in 1970, the middle of my fourth grade year. It was a traumatic event for all involved, as we were the first on both sides of the family to leave the Buffalo area. Within nine months, my parents were getting a divorce. I was the oldest child and only girl and wound up shouldering a lot of my parents' anger, bitterness, and hurt, simply because I was an available ear for each of them. With my extended family support system a state away, I felt especially alone and vulnerable. At such a young age, I was helpless, confused, and hurting. My father's decisions deeply crushed my identity and esteem as a young girl in 1970—long before divorce and childhood counseling were commonplace.

A decade later, my youngest brother was killed in a car accident, exactly two months to the day he graduated from college. I was devastated and reeled from powerlessness and grief. Four years later, my girlfriend was murdered in her apartment in Washington DC, which is still a cold case today. She was waiting for me to finish defending my graduate thesis, and then we were planning to head to the beach to spend a week relaxing and celebrating my degree. A few years later, I was a single professional relocated to Denver, Colorado, when my grandmother, one of my best friends and former roommate, and my father all died unexpectedly. On three different occasions, within months of one another, I was boarding a plane to return east to attend yet another funeral.

It wasn't until a few years later, when I was introduced professionally to information about goal-setting and how the mind works that I began reflecting on the course of my life. I had considered myself reasonably successful in the sense that I continued to climb the career ladder. My titles, areas of responsibility, and salary grew as I worked my way up within the nonprofit sector. I was a graduate of Leadership Denver and contributed eagerly to Chamber of Commerce activities. But my growth was slow, modest, and something that seemed to "happen" to me, at least that's how I looked at it. Why was I so passive about my future, particularly when I had significant accomplishments, merits, and affirmations from others about my abilities?

I realized as I looked back on my very interesting and eclectic experiences that I viewed life as a random set of events that came upon me. I was reacting to life rather than goal-setting to direct my future. I was allowing life to drag me around and define what I should or should not have. And I lived from the perspective of scarcity, loss, and fear, always "waiting for the next shoe to drop."

As I took time for reflection, I had the revelation that as a young girl I established the subconscious belief that life happens outside your control. And as I grew, that belief was only reinforced—reality as you know it can change with a phone call and a stunned voice on the other end telling you someone you love is gone. Without realizing it, I had spent thirty-some years living passively under an external locus of control. Sure, I had hopes and dreams, but I didn't let myself want too much. I had developed a worldview that it didn't make much sense to set goals for yourself when life could change on a dime.

Had I not slowed down enough to take serious time for reflection and had I not come to this revelation about my thinking and how I was living my life, I would not have been able to see the possibilities, choices, and opportunities that were right before me. Had I not released the emotional pain and fear that dominated my life and realigned my thinking to become more positive, constructive, and proactive, I would have been the type of person who heard devastating news about my diagnosis and then delivered my fate into the hands of the doctors, leaving myself vulnerable to their view of my future.

Self-reflective individuals are consciously aware of when they are getting stuck in that external thinking trap. They develop and maintain a tight rein on a mind-set that, in spite of external circumstances, says, "If it's to be, it's up to me." That's not to dismiss or minimize the sovereign power of God but rather to emphasize the personal responsibility and accountability we have for our own choices. Resilient, faith-filled individuals don't let external limitations define or deter their internal vision of hope, victory, or achievement. They won't give in, and they don't give up. They always find a way.

Reflection Activity

1. How about you? Who is in charge of your present circumstances? You? Your doctors? Your family? The insurance company? The disease? The Devil? God?
2. Which of the following most sounds like the way you're thinking and talking right now?
    1. "I guess it is what it is. I'll just have to deal with what comes."
    2. "Why do bad things always happen to me?"
    3. "It's in the doctor's hands now."
    4. "All I can do is hope and pray for the best."
    5. "This is not me. I'm healthy and will search out whatever alternatives are available to beat this thing."
3. Ask yourself why you think that way. Search your memory for where that mind-set first originated. It will make a substantial difference as you attempt to move forward.

Your health must be internally driven. In other words, it's not a "wait and see" type of proposition. You must be positioned to advocate for your own healing if you wish to receive it. If you've embraced the gift of choosing life and accepted accountability for receiving your God-given healing, I offer you my most hearty blessing of congratulations. You are well on the way to building a firm foundation toward health and wholeness. If not, it's time to delve deeply to uncover the beliefs, attitudes, and expectations that might be holding you back.

Whether you stand with remarkable resolve or are still on the fence of your future, it is necessary to become aware of the unknown influences at work within you that are impacting your power of perspective and healing. It accounts for why we often fail at New Year's resolutions or lose our drive and motivation to create constructive change in our lives. It all begins with the beliefs you hold inside your mind that you call "truth" or "reality."

Seeing All There is to See

As an infant, you did not have the cognitive development to evaluate, differentiate, or dissect the complexity of circumstances around you. Your first perspectives of the world were formed by responses to your most basic human needs for hunger, thirst, comfort, sleep, and security. If mother was busy, sick, absent, or overwhelmed, you could not judge the situation and respond with thoughtful composure. Empathy, compassion, rationale, understanding, and patience were not part of your capacity at that point. Your sense of the world and how it treated you was based on whether or not you were fed when you got hungry, protected when you got scared, paid attention to when you fussed, and changed when your diapers were full. The more negligent or un-nurturing your environment was, the more your mind recorded negative emotions of fear, loneliness, scarcity, and pain. Conversely, the more positive and nurturing your care, the more your foundation for life began with a sense of safety, love, and abundance. These early experiences were all recorded in your brain and formed the basis for your attitudes and perspective toward life.

As you developed into childhood, people in authority were constantly offering you information and opinions about your behaviors and characteristics, what you could and could not do, what the world was like around you, and what different sorts of people were like. Acknowledging their position of power, you likely accepted the information you were receiving, even if it didn't accurately represent all that was going on, didn't feel very good, or was harmful to you. Because the mind is a literal mechanism and simply records information as it is experienced, your subconscious mind imprinted their opinions as truth. That information, along with the emotional delivery you encountered, was recorded in the neurons of your brain. And the more you dwelled on these messages or the more those ideas were repeated to you or by you, the deeper those ideas formed as beliefs or truths in your mind, becoming your identity, self-concept, or reality.

For instance, if you were constantly told you were bad, shy, lazy, or terrible at math, your juvenile mind likely did not dispute the accuracy of the information, no matter who told it to you. You may not have liked it. It may not have felt very good. But your mind recorded it, creating tapes in your head defining what kind of person you are and what kind of world you live in. The stronger the emotions used to deliver those opinions—good or bad—the deeper the impact was on your subconscious mind. Every belief you hold about yourself or the world around you was formed in this manner. You perceived it, sanctioned it, recorded it, and through repetition by your own thoughts plus the comments of others, you built beliefs that were etched into the neural pathways of your brain. Can you think of some early beliefs you have right now that are no longer serving you well?

The reason this is of such consequence is science has proven that these tapes, or truths, you have stored in your subconscious mind determine your behavior and outcomes in life far more than your conscious-level willpower. Willpower is effective as long as you have the stamina, focus, and fortitude to keep your constant conscious attention and efforts on your desired goals. But the minute you get tired, busy, under stress, preoccupied, or go "back to normal," you automatically revert back to the dominant beliefs and images you hold in your subconscious mind and behave according to who you know yourself to be—good or bad, effective or inefficient, healthy or diseased. As you confront new situations on a momentary basis, you automatically respond in agreement with your stored "truths."

And they don't change unless you identify the specific belief holding you back (revelation) and deliberately form new, more positive and constructive truths (realignment) to replace the ones limiting the use of the true potential inside you (restoration).

So if the information you've received along your journey of life that has influenced your ideas of truth was anything *but* true, wouldn't you see that by now? Not necessarily. Could you be missing opportunities and under-living your life's purpose, potential, and performance? You bet. Could it deter or undermine your hope for healing? For sure.

The purpose of this book is to help you identify and reprogram those archaic, ineffective, life-threatening beliefs that just aren't true. As you learn to navigate your mind, you'll see how you receive information, how you evaluate decisions, and how you respond to truth subconsciously may be the very root of dis-ease you've been experiencing in your life and body.

Why Our Senses Don't Always Make Sense

Have you ever tried to explain a concept or get your point of view across to someone and they just couldn't "see" it? No matter how hard you tried or emphatic your delivery, they just didn't get it? Have you ever wondered why something can be so obvious to you but remains absolutely oblivious to your kids, spouse, or colleagues? Have you ever known someone to be so opinionated that they don't see any other alternative besides their own, even when that alternative is staring them right in the face?

You might be inclined to think these people are obstinate, ornery folks who would like nothing more than to make your life miserable. And perhaps they are! But in most cases, what they're experiencing is a sensory blocking out of information that actually exists. It's a common occurrence that happens to all of us all the time—we're simply not aware of it. We always think we're seeing all there is to see.

A classic illustration of this psychological and physiological phenomenon is one The Pacific Institute has used for many years in their work with building high-performance organizations. The example is reflected in the sentence below. Try your hand at this by reading the following sentence *one time* out loud to yourself:

FINISHED FILES ARE THE RESULT OF YEARS OF SCIENTIFIC STUDY COMBINED WITH THE EXPERIENCE OF MANY YEARS OF EXPERTS.

Stop there! Don't try to analyze or memorize the sentence. Just go back and read the sentence once through again. Only this time as you read it, count the number of <u>F</u>s you read along the way.

How many did you find?

Two? Three? Six? More?

The fact is there are seven Fs in the sentence above. If you didn't find them all the first time, read the sentence out loud this time and try even harder!

Got all seven?

If you still don't, try counting the Fs in the words *of.* Now do you see them all?

When I do this exercise live in a group, inevitably more than half the room misses a few Fs along the way. It evokes lots of laughter, wonderment, and a bit of embarrassment. It's amazing how a room full of people could all be staring at the same thing but seeing different results—even when I have them go back and search a second and third time. To de-escalate any awkwardness or embarrassment, I quickly let them know the better reader they are, the more inclined they would be to miss the Fs in the word *of.*

It's not because it's a small or insignificant word, which is the response most people give for the large-scale oversight. It has to do with our past conditioning. If you learned English as your formative language growing up, you would have learned it phonetically where *of* is pronounced "o-v." Since we don't actually see words with our eyes—we only pick up light with our eyes and translate that light bounced off of stored pictures or images in our mind—our past conditioning (reading and pronunciation, in this case) will cause us to overlook the Fs in words where the F is pronounced like a V.

The F sentence is a fun, eye-opening illustration that shows how we visually block out information that's actually there. But the same is true for our other senses of sound, touch, taste, and smell.

Our senses don't give us the whole picture. And yet our modern, enlightened, scientific world has us rely on our natural sensory perception to experience, make sense of, and validate the world around us. We form our very pictures, ideals, and beliefs on what we perceive with our senses. So why is this so important and relevant to healing?

Since childhood, the foundation for our ideas of truth and reality began by accepting or sanctioning the ideas and opinions given to us by the "authorities" in our lives. Teachers, coaches, older siblings, the big kids, parents, bosses, and doctors all influenced our perspective of our self and our world based on what they perceived as truth. But we're not necessarily seeing the whole truth; we filter out information that actually exists. There's more sight, sound, smell, touch, taste, possibility, answers, solutions, and realities than we've yet to perceive or even discover. So we shouldn't be so quick to accept the "truth" about our condition or ourselves from others, particularly when that truth is limiting or harmful or works against our goal of healing.

Case in point: The medical community works diligently to save lives. Doctors spend years of study and practice and oodles of money in education, malpractice insurance, and other business-related costs to practice and live by their Hippocratic Oath. Meanwhile, advances in diagnoses, procedures, and supplemental therapies occur daily. Most of these people are wonderful, dedicated professionals who commit their lives to your well-being. But it's also essential to consider that their specialized education and approach only consider sickness and treatment through one lens—traditional medicine.

Pharmacology and Western medicine is only one approach to healing. For decades, their most effective means of treating aggressive cancers has been in the form of poisoning the body with chemotherapy, which destroys both bad and good cells and suppresses the very thing that keeps us healthy in the first place, our immune system. Doctors have little to no training in nutrition and the body's ability to restore and renew itself. For years, I had been taking supplements doctors dismissed as a waste of effort and money. Today, some of these very vitamins and minerals like CoQ10, Omega 3, and Vitamin D3 are promoted within mainstream Western medicine. What other natural regenerative options are just waiting in the wings for the nod of approval? (More on this in *The Body to Heal*.)

Yesterday's improbabilities become today's baseline for diagnosis and treatment. It's important to consider that pharmacology's propping up of Western medicine doesn't necessarily constitute the corner on truth as it relates to the body's ability to adapt and heal.

Along those same lines, medical professionals are not theologians or spiritual counselors who prescribe the power of faith or any of the healing promises God has given us. And while they may ascent to the fact that optimistic patients who take care of themselves fare better than those who are not, and though studies coming out of the halls of academia demonstrate people of faith and in faith communities heal better than those who are not, there are few medical institutions who integrate this kind of holistic approach to restoring your health. What if they're only seeing three Fs when there's opportunity here and opportunity there? Will they see it even if you present them with alternative evidence? Not if they've built a strong belief in their traditional way as the only legitimate way. If you build the belief there is no way, you'll block out all other ways. That's how the mind works. We always think what we're seeing is the truth.

The physiology of this phenomenon takes place where your cerebral cortex is connected to your brain stem. It's called the Reticular Activating System (RAS) and it plays a primary role for your awareness and thinking abilities, filtering or screening out information you deem unimportant or insignificant. It's an important function in that you could not possibly focus if your brain tried to receive all the sensory information actually existing around you at any given moment. There's just too much of it, and you couldn't effectively concentrate.

Your RAS only processes two kinds of information: threatening and purposeful. All other information is blocked out. So when you know *of* is pronounced "o-v," the Reticular Activating System will block out the Fs in *of*. When you *know* your kids are messy, you've lost the keys to your car, life is unfair, or disease is consuming your body, your creative subconscious mind has the job of making you look sane for believing what you believe. And it does so by the RAS allowing in only information that is congruent with your existing beliefs and filters out all other information, including any time the kids pick up their things. Yet it takes in all the information you need to confirm your beliefs every time the kids don't live up to your standards.

When you understand the power of perspective and how the Reticular Activating System filters out any information that conflicts with the existing beliefs you hold, it should inevitably lead you to an important insight about your worldview and your healing: "If my past conditioning impacts my beliefs, and those beliefs impact what information my RAS takes in, what else might I be missing? What have I been leaving out in life? What opportunities have I dismissed or overlooked simply because I couldn't see them at the time?"

Reflection Activity

1. As you read through the F-card exercise, past conditioning, the power of perspective, and the Reticular Activating System, what revelations surfaced about your own life and your own thinking?
2. In what areas of your life (spiritual, physical, emotional, financial, educational, relational, etc.) might your past conditioning be impacting how you're handling your

current situation? List each area and describe the beliefs you hold relative to your condition.

3. Where do these beliefs come from? Whose voice do you hear?

4. How might these beliefs be limiting you from receiving your healing?

Trapped in the Rearview Mirror ...

Perspective is a choice. You alone determine and are responsible for how you will respond to any given moment. But perspective, once fully formed as a belief in your mind, becomes encoded into the neurons of your brain and becomes part of your psychological DNA. It becomes your "truth" or "reality" as you see it, even if it doesn't fully or accurately represent the complete picture of the situation, even if it is spiritually, physically, or emotionally harmful to you. It becomes your subconscious, automatic, programmed response unless or until you consciously decide to change it.

From in utero to present, your senses—sight, sound, smell, touch, taste—have been gathering and imprinting information in the neurons of your brain, storing every bit on the subconscious level. As you encounter new information, challenges, experiences, and opportunities, you don't respond to them in a vacuum. Your mind automatically and instantaneously activates a four-step decision-making process using past information and experiences stored in your subconscious mind.

- In Step One of the decision-making process, you experience conscious-level awareness, perception, or observation of information coming to you through your senses of sight, sound, smell, taste, and touch.
- In Step Two, your mind bounces that sensory data off your subconscious library of stored memory. It's looking for instances of familiarity or similarity between what you are currently experiencing and what you've experienced

in the past. In essence, your mind is asking the question, "Do I have any context, relationship, or association with this new information? Does this resemble anything I've seen, felt, tasted, smelled, or experienced in the past?"

- If the answer is "Yes, this does remind me of a former experience," your mind begins to extrapolate and transfer the former outcomes from your stored memory to your potential new outcomes. In Step Three, you begin to estimate, on a subconscious level, the probabilities of whether your new situation will be helpful or harmful, good or bad, easy or hard, successful or failed, and so on, based on your former experiences.

- The stronger the emotion tied to your former experience, the greater the likelihood you will lean favorably toward or fearfully away from this "similar" new opportunity. Step Four is where the conscious-level decision is made.

Why is this so significant? Because unless you are aware of how your mind works, you may unconsciously base your future, not on the potential of what could be, but on your history of what has been. And while this may be quite helpful in certain circumstances—let's face it, how many times do you need to touch a hot stove or iron to learn the heated metal consumes your skin?—in most cases, it limits what you can be, see, or have. Think back to one of your more recent experiences, like when you were given your prognosis.

Doctors are immersed daily in the world of diagnoses, disease, and death. It's the lens through which they operate. The past histories of others form the basis for your future. It's a "reality" trap that often skews doctors' perspectives.

When I was at a highly acclaimed cancer institute for my third opinion on an incurable metastasized cancer, I was told by the doctor that, based on my diagnosis and the historical data of others, I would have about one year before the current treatment would be rendered ineffective, and we would be looking at the cancer spreading to other organs in my body.

Not a single time, with any of the doctors I saw, did they look at my fitness, my mind-set, my heart, my faith, and my nutrition and factor in the potential of what could be. Nor did they ask me what I could do to give healing a chance to take root in my body. That's not to say none noted my "cheery disposition" on the medical records. But I was told it was better to be "realistic" and not to be given "false hope." My fate was packaged not in the potential of what could be but on the history of what had been for others. I felt stalled between the doctor's rearview statistics of death behind me and the horizon of healing before me.

Certainly history is an important benchmark for us on so many levels. But we need to be consciously aware of when it is protecting us from harm or robbing us of hope.

Reflection Activity

1. What hurts, fears, disappointments, or shame have you experienced in life that are still impacting how you make decisions today?
2. Think of a time when you passed up a great opportunity or relationship because you were looking back in the past of what had been rather than toward the potential of what could be. What happened?
3. Knowing what you now know about the decision-making process, how might you begin to improve the quality of your decisions?
4. Gives examples of that improvement for your health and healing.

Living a Life of Miracles

There is a noteworthy principle long established among cognitive scientists, "We don't get what we want; we get what we expect," otherwise known as the Self-Fulfilling Prophecy. If we expect a bad day, our Reticular Activating System will pick up evidence of it everywhere, or we'll subconsciously sabotage circumstances to cause bad things to happen for us. If we expect to get sick, psychoneuroimmunology is proving we can actually weaken our immune system, increasing stress and inflammation through worry and negative goal setting. If we don't expect to do well on an interview, we can cause ourselves to feel so out of our comfort zone that we will appear nervous, tongue-tied, sweaty, insecure, and unprepared. We draw people, resources, and opportunities to ourselves we feel worthy of receiving. In the same way, we subconsciously push away people, resources, and opportunities we feel are not worthy of us—good *and* bad. As a result, we wind up living not at our level of potential but at our level of expectation. Our ceiling for what's possible is set at our belief level of what is truth or "reality" for us.

If you are familiar with missionary efforts in developing, third-world regions, you may have heard of amazing incidences of miraculous healings. And while you may question the legitimacy of these miracles, I can tell you I personally know individuals who travel abroad as part of faith-based and medical missionary teams who have witnessed a lame man walking, sight restored to the blind, and the deaf who now hear. It's absolutely incredible to the modern mind ... and therein lays the problem. Our sophisticated modern world no longer views life through a spiritual lens, which sees and attracts the miraculous.

Lest we thoughtlessly and unconsciously adopt this prevailing secular view, it's important to see how our industrialized thinking has progressed, or more nearly regressed, over the centuries. In any age and in every century, there has been pagan unbelief competing against God and the supernatural in the mainstream society. But the Enlightenment of the eighteenth century caused a tremendous shift on the philosophical, social, and scientific cultures of the industrial world. Science, reason, and logic began to displace and eventually supersede what had been a predominantly spiritual perspective that acknowledged and accepted the supernatural influence over our daily lives. Where the great social and scientific minds to this point had used their efforts to search out an understanding of God and the heavens, the Enlightenment heightened the credibility of those who sought to explain and exalt the nature of man.

As science and philosophy detached further and further from faith, we began to disengage our sixth sense, handicapping the experience and perception of the spiritual realm. This new Age of Reason scoffed at those who endorsed the supernatural as uneducated, fundamentalist, or superstitious. If something could not be verified, it could not be validated. More and more, the enlightened world began to darken its spiritual eyes, even within the church where the miraculous apparently ended with the last page of our biblical narrative and the beginning of the church age.

As we moved toward modernity, God and spiritual reality were confined deeper behind the four walls of the church or synagogue and politely removed from political, educational, and social sectors. Objective truth lost its grounding as the postmodern world drove an even wider wedge between the public and private self, claiming what was thought and done in seclusion had no impact on one's public performance. This schizophrenic ideology opened the door to all types of "personal liberties" on the social agenda without fully comprehending the incongruities and consequences on cognitive thinking. The result was we continued to dissect ourselves and deteriorate the alignment of spirit, mind, and body that result in our health and wholeness.

In a shrinking world of so many options, tolerance for everyone's subjective inclinations became more important than the wisdom and power of ancient revelation. With no real substance other than personal preference to support it, we adopted a salad-bar mentality around spirituality. A bit of this and a bit of that to suit our own appetites and agendas flipped our thinking and insights on its head. Rather than live from our true identity in the Spirit, which transforms our thinking and manifests in our physical, psychological, and spiritual lives, we have elevated personal preferences and desires to shape our thinking and rationalize our worldview. We call it "freedom" and proclaim "the sky's the limit," but we miss the irony as we confine our lives within the walls of the natural realm and stunt our possibilities by the makings of our own understanding. Our wisdom is foolishness to God (1 Corinthians 1:20).

Living a life of miracles is all about expectations where faith— "being *sure* of what we hope for and *certain* of what we do not see," Hebrews 11:1(emphasis mine)—is the major currency in God's economy. It's not about being good enough to receive, it's not about praying for things and waiting to see what happens, it's not about a vending-machine universe existing to fulfill our every attraction. It's about a sure and steady confidence in God's character, power, promises, and provision for them who believe. To live a life of miracles, we must recapture a heavenly perspective or, as the writer of Corinthians puts it, "have the mind of Christ" (1 Corinthians 2:16).

I have a wonderfully creative and zany friend, Teresa, who naturally lives her life this way. Her confident relationship with God, knowledge of His Word, and anticipation of His provision enable her to live with an expanding expectation of what He will do for her each day. Miracles, or what others might refer to as "coincidences," seem to happen around every bend. She consistently embraces life through a heavenly perspective, even in the small things, and sees rich symbolism in what most of us would otherwise overlook. As a result, these manifestations of God create deeper faith that begets more miracles that establish higher expectations for how God will involve Himself in her life. She walks in a level of faith, trust, and relationship that is brow-raising to most. But the miracles in her life are fascinating, enviable, and undeniable.

By contrast, I've encountered situations where God is clearly answering prayer in people's lives, but because they view circumstances from the natural realm, they miss their miracle and don't grow in their faith. Using medicine, science, reason, or logic, they explain away the blessing rather than receive and rejoice in what could be theirs.

I most recently experienced this with a dear loved one, a forty-year veteran of type-one, juvenile diabetes. Since her early thirties, her life and body have been plagued with medical mishaps attributed to those with brittle, uncontrollable blood sugars. Over the years, I've marveled at how resilient she has been in body and spirit, in many cases defying the odds for someone who has had such a severe case for so very long. Though I pray for her health and protection regularly, I've asked God, in light of my own healing, if He would restore a pancreas that hasn't worked for more than half a life. More than mercifully keep her in sound health, could He actually reverse type-one, juvenile diabetes?

A resurgence of dangerously low blood sugar levels and an emergency hospital visit prompted another appointment with her endocrinologist. Her doctor was ecstatic to report A1C sugar levels (the amount of blood sugars showing up in the body) at 7.5, where 7.0 is the desired norm. What makes this so amazing is her levels had never been even close to that number in her entire diabetic life! The doctor drastically cut back the amount of regular insulin she'd been receiving from her pump. She's on a record low level of insulin since age thirty-three. That alone is worthy of a "hallelujah," as now she does not have to eat just to keep up with insulin requirements, as she found herself doing.

When I shared my belief in God's healing taking place over her, I sensed cautious optimism. Although she's a person of faith and had been religiously reading the Scripture affirmations of healing from *The Spirit to Heal*, the identity of being an incurable diabetic for so long was more real to her than the God who could restore a dead pancreas—after all, that just doesn't happen in our world. I reminded her not to be so dismissive about what's happening in her body.

Living a life of miracles involves us acknowledging, apprehending, and appreciating daily occurrences with a heavenly perspective. Like toning our bodies, it requires flexing our spiritual muscles on a regular basis so we are not crushed under the weight of the world's afflictions or diverted by constant distractions. Thankfully, growing in expectant faith is not dependent on us alone. It is the Spirit that communicates with our spirit to guide us into all truth and remind us of our heavenly potential.

For the past few years, my husband and I considered moving across the river to the other part of the metropolitan area. Though we were still fresh in our beautiful custom-built home I designed and decorated and were enjoying the most wonderful neighborhood of friends we had ever experienced, we kept thinking the locale and county weren't where our lives were heading. We often scoured the home sale listings and occasionally drove neighborhoods to see if there was one particular area that compelled us. It was hard to find anything we liked better than our own house and always chose to stay put. At one point, we put our house on the market for a few months but found people enjoyed coming to look at our award-winning home more than wanting to buy it. The inconvenience of cleaning and showing our home and finding a place to camp out while potential buyers meandered about was more than we could tolerate.

After the second diagnosis and healing, I felt an even stronger prompting to move across the river, only this time it was to reduce our footprint and purge ourselves of the things and lifestyle stealing our time, attention, resources, and God-given purpose. I found myself one morning worrying with God over the logistics of a move—when and where, selling our home first or finding another. In my stress and anxiety, the Spirit brought to mind my friend Teresa and the many miracles around selling and buying her homes. He also spoke gently into my heart, saying, "Really? Haven't you learned by now? If God could heal your body of incurable cancer, don't you think He could sell your house if you released it to Him?" I actually laughed aloud at my own omission and then approached God with bold expectation. As if to affirm my own faith, I audibly confessed that if God could do miracles for Teresa, I knew He could do them for me. If making a move was His will for us as I sensed it was, and if He could heal me from stage four metastasized breast cancer, He could easily bring someone to my door who wanted to buy my house *without* even listing our property, putting a sign in the yard, and scheduling around multiple showings.

I released the stress and worry and trusted He would do it in His perfect timing. And He did … within the next few weeks! No sign … no listing our property … no multiple showings. More than that, the new buyer was totally flexible with his move-in date, allowing us the freedom to work with our son's school schedule. He even wanted to buy much of my furniture, items I didn't want or need in our new downscaled home. God did exceedingly abundantly more than all I could ask or imagine, not because He's some genie in a bottle waiting to fulfill my every whim, but because, in His will, He is good and delights in giving good gifts to His children. When we trust in His goodness, we open our mind, heart, and awareness to receiving and living a life of miracles.

The challenge we face is living day-to-day in the paradox of two real and seemingly opposing realms—the heavenly realm, or things of the Spirit, and the earthy realm, or things of the natural—where our mind is the gateway between each of these dominions. Either we entertain the purposes and potential of heaven or the ideals and attitudes of the here and now. The direction our mind swings and what we focus upon determine what we see and experience.

This occurs as a result of another important principle of cognitive psychology: *The human mind cannot hold two conflicting thoughts or concepts at the same time without stress and anxiety occurring.* We often experience this type of dis-ease when confronted with paradox. One of the functions of our creative subconscious is to minimize stress and restore order to our thinking whenever it senses conflict or anxiety arising. Interestingly, the mind is amoral and doesn't care in which direction it restores the order. It doesn't pause and argue with us when we're heading in the wrong direction. The mind simply gravitates toward the ideals most consistent with the beliefs, attitudes, habits, and expectations we already hold in our subconscious mind.

Because one set of ideas will feel more "comfortable" than the other, we conclude it must be truth, while the other side is wrong. The mind simply seeks resolution and moves us toward the most dominant idea we already possess—our version of the truth.

As we gravitate toward one realm, we automatically block out information or evidence of the other. What we see is what we get. We move toward what we think about. That's how the mind works. And our physiology follows.

If we think miracles, we open our perspective to see miracles. If we meditate on the things of heaven, we build a heavenly expectation and acquire qualities and characteristics that allow us to tackle life issues above the fray.

"For though we live in the world, we do not wage war as the world does. The weapons we fight with are not the weapons of this world. On the contrary, they have divine power to demolish strongholds. We demolish arguments and every pretension that sets itself up against the knowledge of God, and we take captive every thought to make it obedient to Christ" (2 Corinthians 10:4–5).

But if we dwell exclusively on truth as the current reality we experience in the natural realm, as defined by time, space, and substance, then we live in the midst of our circumstances and replicate the here and now. The best we have is to hope for the best.

Living a life of miracles is not about choosing one reality and ignoring the other but realizing both exist and impact the truth and life we live. As we encounter life issues, our conscious approach should not be either/or but both/and. When we understand the holistic, redeeming nature of the gospel, we see it is through the paradoxes of life that God brings about meaning, wholeness, healing, sufficiency, and restoration:

- We must die to live
- We are sinners yet redeemed
- We relinquish to receive

- We become last to be first
- We live freely in God's sovereignty

It is where we choose to position ourselves that determines our perspective and release of potential in any given situation. We live either from our earthly circumstances or our heavenly inheritance, not because we think positively but because it is Christ who holds all things together (Colossians 1:17), past, present, future, natural and supernatural.

This revelation in the midst of my own battle provided me with permission to be so bold and confident about my healing before I had any physical evidence it was taking place. I recognized the doctors' diagnoses; I just didn't accept them as the only reality for my life. I knew there was another truth or perspective, stronger and more established, to battle the strongholds against my health. Armed with the Word of God and what He says about His nature and provision for those who trust, I was able to live in the paradox of both realities—disease and healing—and align myself with life through the healing promises of God in Christ Jesus (see Book One, *The Spirit to Heal*).

The real battle was keeping my mind fixed and unwavering on those promises and making sure my self-talk, both aloud and to myself, was consistent with those beliefs. Let's face it, we do live and move and have our being in the here and now. We feel pain and experience trauma. As long as we have breath on this earth, we live in the natural realm. The idea is not to dismiss one for the other but to expand our understanding and embrace the marvel and mystery of paradox. It's then we see paradox no longer as oppositional conflict but as complementary dualities, the yin and yang of creation and its Creator. In our weakness, He is strong.

We know by now that the problem with perspective is, although we think we're always seeing the truth, our mind doesn't allow us to grasp all the realities that actually exist. On a physiological level (the body), the Reticular Activating System filters out information that's actually there but we subconsciously deem non-essential to us, leaving out Fs here and there from our perspective. On a psychological level (the mind), our past conditioning and subconscious beliefs and attitudes influence the lens through which we receive, interpret, and respond to existing information. On a spiritual level, we are so malnourished from centuries of neglect or religiosity that the eyes of our heart dim the realities of the supernatural realm. And yet our rational, intellectual, scientific minds always think we're seeing the truth.

Living a life of miracles takes believing, but it's so much more than cognitive conviction. Kathryn Kuhlman, miracle healer of the 1950s, wrote in her book *I Believe in Miracles*, that you can believe a promise and at the same time not have the faith to seize it. Where *belief* is a cognitive or mental condition, faith is a living, vibrant revelation imparted to us by God, the author and perfector of our faith.

Living a life of miracles is full of limitless potential when we harness the power of perspective and understand the natural realm is not the final word on truth and life. Living a life of miracles begins with revelation in the Spirit, relationship in God's goodness and power, and receptivity to the things of heaven in the here and now. And this life in the Spirit always lives from who we are—our identity in potential—in Christ Jesus.

Reflection Activity

1. What is your biggest roadblock to apprehending more of the miraculous in your life? Why do you feel that way, and where did the belief(s) originate?
2. If you would like to live a life of miracles, ask God to open and enlighten the eyes of your spiritual heart and increase your faith. Do it now, and begin to look for His activity in your life.

3. In James 1, we are told that if any of us lacks wisdom, we should ask God who gives generously without finding fault. But when we ask, we must believe and not doubt, otherwise God sees us as double-minded and unstable, and we should not think we will receive anything from Him. What areas of your life would you like more wisdom? List them specifically. Invite God to give you His perspective—the mind of Christ—for each of these areas of need.

4. If your thoughts, words, and actions embraced more of the miraculous, what would look differently in your pursuit of healing?

Picture Perfect:
Creating Health and Wellness in the Midst of Disease

Blog Entry: May 31, 2009

Setting Sails

"You cannot change the wind, but you can redirect your sails."

Rehoboth Beach was a godsend for me. No one knew me. I didn't have to talk about cancer. My tube was gone. And except for the tenderness and numbing around and under my right arm, I was essentially on my way to wholeness.

This was the second time my parents had bid on and won this weekend condo from one of their fundraising events. What was especially fun for me was this last weekend before the official season began was Sidewalk Sale Weekend. Racks and tables of merchandise lined the streets, luring hungry bargain hunters inside for more. Other than the obligatory tourist sweatshirt (purchased in Olympic time), Brent, my dad, and Nicholas would have none of it. They tore off to the beach for kite flying and Frisbee.

One of my favorite shops was a shabby chic boutique selling everything from small pieces of furniture to handmade soaps. Sections were thoughtfully themed, making meandering both an adventure and a challenge to absorb it all. In one cozy corner, a nautical collection caught my eye. Dominating the space was a gilt-framed blackboard that was freestanding and leaning against the wall. The chalked inscription read, "You cannot change the wind, but you can redirect your sails." I exhaled a knowing "Amen" and mused over the new waters I was traveling this time around.

My last fight in 2006 was just that … a fight. I armed myself with healing Scriptures, a firm mind-set, a more holistic lifestyle, and a heaping dose of self-reliance: "If it's to be, it's up to me." I didn't allow for much intervention on the part of friends and family. I would be just fine; we didn't need meals or carpooling arrangements. Nicholas was starting kindergarten four days after my surgery, and I was determined to get over it and take him to his first day of school. I worked hard to "believe" the right things (which really isn't belief at all if you have to work so hard at it), say the right things, and show others as well as myself that I was a survivor. My militant attitude was so strong that it wasn't more than a week after finishing thirty-three days of radiation and I signed up to run a half marathon in NYC. I couldn't even run to the end of the block at that point, not to mention I had never run more than four miles before—and that was ten years earlier. In typical fashion, I set my sails directly into the wind, poised for a fight.

This time has been different yet so much harder for me. Instead of battling directly into the wind, I've let myself be carried along by the fullness that fills my sails. At the wise and loving insistence of my sweet friend Cathy, I promised to sit back, relax, and receive. No fighting, no rugged individualism, no superwoman tactics … just "yes" and "thank you" and allowing myself to be loved. Following surgery, Cathy coordinated eight days of meals to arrive at our home. My neighborhood and fellowship group girlfriends took turns delivering delicious, healthy meals. Brent and I marveled at just how fabulous vegetables, fish, and chicken could taste. I have to believe they were pulling out all the stops; otherwise, I'd be absolutely demoralized as a cook and abandon my kitchen forever.

Cards, prayers, e-mails, flowers, books and CDs came, filling me with such gratitude for the amazing people who have been woven into my life. Last week, I was emotionally hijacked when a gift certificate arrived for many weeks of gourmet catering given by families in Nicholas's second grade. It was the first time I sat and sobbed uncontrollably, feeling humbled and undeserving. It's been hard and highly uncomfortable being the center of attention in this way (because "really, I'm just not that helpless"), but I truly have seen the hands and heart of God through the people in my life. So let the winds stir. My sails are full while charting still waters.

Healing hugs,
Doreen

Choose Potential:
Living a Life of Inheritance

IT WAS 2007, AND I was working with one of the low-income, inner-city Philadelphia public schools. I was teaching high performance concepts to create more effective teaching to the faculty and staff of this elementary school. The teachers were given this opportunity to reflect on how the daily socioeconomic challenges they faced were impacting their teaching, student behavior, and school culture. Many revealing moments surfaced when teachers and staff discovered beliefs that were lowering their expectations of students, the school district, and themselves.

The next step was teaching them how to uproot these limiting beliefs and how to create new neural pathways in the mind more in line with their desired outcomes. This would enable them to create the change they wanted from the inside out, allowing their new behaviors to flow freely from their fresh thinking, thus eliminating the constant stress and pressure of trying harder to be more positive and constructive. Through a process of realignment, they created and then assimilated new belief statements describing the potential outcomes they desired as if they were already accomplished in the present. For instance, if a teacher discovered that he held prejudices about certain students with particular attributes and realized those subconscious beliefs were negatively impacting his expectations and attitudes toward those students, a new belief was created which would yield more effective results, i.e., "I find the star quality in each individual student. My teaching creatively draws out their greatness."

As they moved from reflection to revelation to realignment, a particular male teacher became unusually uncooperative. Acknowledging his frustration, I allowed him the opportunity to vent. After several minutes of ramble, we were able to unravel the root of his concern. The notion of realigning his beliefs, habits, attitudes, and expectations to be more consistent with who he is in potential was unconscionable to him. He repeatedly argued that to do so would be confessing a lie. He could not affirm in the present tense positive, more constructive, and effective attributes about himself if he currently didn't possess them. The whole concept to him felt disingenuous. He was so entrenched in the perspective and reality of the here and now that he simply could not see the validity and freedom of living from potential and new beginnings. Though he willingly confessed self-imposed limitations that stunted his own life, he couldn't and wouldn't grasp the power and perspective of paradox—understanding that both realities exist simultaneously, and that it's his choice to affirm in which direction he will focus his mind. So he chose "today."

Documented studies on the mind and human behavior show we use between 10 and 20 percent of our potential. For more than sixty years, the science of the mind (cognitive psychology), social learning theory, and the neurosciences have attempted to discover and define processes for unleashing more of that unlimited brain power and raw potential in order to achieve higher levels of true success and self-actualization.

According to research, potential in any area of our lives is influenced by three primary factors:

1. our genetic makeup, or our "first nature,"
2. our past conditioning, including all our experiences, environments, and education, or what is called our "second nature," and

3. how we make choices and enact them into our daily lives; what cognitive scientists call "human agency"

Of the three factors, the one over which we have most control and influence is human agency. One of the pioneers of human agency in social cognitive theory is Dr. Albert Bandura of Stanford University. For decades, he has produced volumes of work on the nature and function of self-belief or "efficacy" in human behavior.

According to Bandura, our internal beliefs about our own ability to cause or make things happen are the critical elements determining how we respond to life circumstances on a daily basis. These instantaneous self-assessments about our abilities, positive or negative, happen on the subconscious level and determine the release of our potential at any given moment and in any given area of our lives.

So if we believe we are horrible at public speaking, we will avoid any opportunity to do so. If we find ourselves forced into a position where we must address a group in public, our self-belief about how terrible we are will create so much discomfort and anxiety that it will impact our physiology and performance. We will perspire, appear nervous, feel insecure, and get tongue-tied. All the information about the topic we thoroughly knew when rehearsing to ourselves gets lost in recall. We observe our fear and stumbling and then reinforce our belief about how bad we are with more evidence and conviction. This confirmation, along with the emotional damage, builds stronger and deeper beliefs limiting the use of our potential in the area of public speaking. An internal process of self-regulation keeps us at this same general level of performance—even if we perform better the next time—unless or until we change the underlying beliefs about our abilities in that area. We must change the internal idea of who we are and what we can do. Why? Because when the stress and tension of trying harder causes us to give up conscious control of the change we're trying to make, we always go back to behaving like the person our subconscious mind knows us to be. Over the course of your life, in which areas have you tried to be better than you believe yourself to be? What were the results?

What Bandura's work on efficacy revealed is we can feel highly confident or causative about particular areas of our lives while having low self-efficacy in other areas. Unlike self-esteem, which tends to be a pervasive value we place over our entire being, efficacy is task specific. We can feel great about ourselves in one particular area but lousy about ourselves in another. And with the proper understanding of the human mind and behavior, we can develop our efficacy and release untapped potential in any area in which we desire an upgrade in our level of performance.

Interestingly, the source or "fount" of this unlimited potential we seem to possess remains the great unknown and unnamed in all this scientific research. While scientific, earthbound thinking easily distinguishes our uniquely human capabilities from those of animals, it falls short when explaining the origins, parameters, and characteristics of true potential. As happened with the male teacher from Philadelphia, without a proper perspective, living from potential can feel like a baseless form of positive thinking or hyped-up self-help.

Though I tried to address his concerns with all the appropriate, inclusive, politically correct jargon expected of me in this professional setting, I desperately needed the language of the heart—faith—to help him see the bigger picture. Yes, if we are solely defined by the present here and now, if we are limited by "seeing is believing," then creating and assimilating desired outcomes as if they are achieved statements of fact *is* a lie, nothing more than pie-in-the-sky wishful thinking. We are merely duping ourselves into believing more than evidence shows we can accomplish. As long as we stay stuck in "it is what it is" reality, our tomorrows look all too similar to today. We blindly accept and live in the mediocrity of mind, body, and spirit and keep ourselves from the powerful destiny God purposed for each one of us.

Fortunately, that is not our only option. Instead of striving toward hopeful possibilities, we can thrive in certain potential—a potential that has its origins and existence in the heart of the Creator. We have been given a spiritual identity just as we have a physical identity. Our spirit responds according to spiritual law just as our bodies function under natural law. Spiritual law provides access to an inheritance available for those who will believe and receive. It's a gift of God, so no man or woman might boast of his or her own doing. Its genius arises out of the inextinguishable love and strategic grace of a God who planned for us to exist with Him in the relationship of glory for all eternity, even when none of us was qualified to do so.

I Am as "I AM"

At the dawn of creation, God made light from darkness, order from chaos, and matter from nothingness. The precision and intricacies and interdependencies observed throughout all life and space were materialized out of the proclamations of the almighty God. He spoke, "Let there be light," and creation was established. Life was in the power of His spoken Word. And made in His image, He also gave our utterances the power to create life or death (Proverbs 18:21).

As God established relationship with those who would have a heart of faith and trust toward Him, He set them apart with a new identity and a new inheritance. In Exodus 3, God appears to Moses in the burning bush and gives him his new destiny. Moses, a fugitive turned shepherd, is called by God to return to the place of his crime and deliver the Israelites out of slavery from the hands of the mighty Egyptians. Moses felt neither qualified nor confident to fulfill his God-given mission, so he presses God for assurance and insurance. In essence, he questions both his capacity and authority—or his efficacy and power—to undertake such a miraculous feat when asked by others to support his claims. To invoke Pharaoh to relinquish and inspire his people to relocate, Moses needed to speak God's identity to be credible and successful in his own destiny. So he asks God what he should say when the Israelites question him about the name of the one who sent him. God defined His name for all eternity and set the parameters for our alignment and inheritance by answering, "I AM WHO I AM…say to the Israelites: I AM has sent me to you." To the degree Moses positioned his spirit, mind, and body to take on the identity, authority, and power of I AM, he accomplished spectacular supernatural feats beyond the scope of what is common to man in the natural realm. God placed a God-deposit in Moses as Moses affirmed the living, life-giving I AM.

Another example of this spiritual inheritance occurs in Genesis 17 where God gives Abram a new identity and purpose as He establishes His covenant relationship with him. God tells him his name is now changed from Abram to Abraham because he will be the father of many nations. Being childless and already in his nineties, Abram was hardly qualified to attain such a lofty position. But God didn't say grow into this stature first, and then I will proclaim this status over you. God gave Abram a new identity and authority to claim before there was any evidence or manifestation of the kind. In faith, Abraham accepted and affirmed the promises of God, which we see credited to him as "righteousness" (Genesis 15:6).

Every time Abram declared himself as Abraham, he confirmed his potential, identity, and alignment with God, the almighty, everlasting I AM. Abraham was affirming the deposit I AM placed in him rather than the natural circumstances that were presently surrounding him as an elderly, fatherless man. A piece of God's character—righteousness—was given to Abraham as he aligned himself in faith with God's word to him. And we have been given that same opportunity to either align our identity—our "I am's"— with the God of creation to accomplish things on Earth as they are in heaven or to align our "I am's" with the things of this natural and decaying world.

Before the world began, God foreknew our actions and the consequences of the free will He would program into our DNA. And though love motivates mutual consent, justice requires retribution. All along, God's divine strategy allowed for us to love or reject freely while, at the same time, deliver us from eternal death and darkness, which is the result of our choices to live apart from Him. God doesn't outrightly pardon our guilt. There is no justice in that. It's the law of cause and effect; actions beget consequences. Someone must stand trial and account for the crime. So the paradox of justice and mercy were nailed together on the cross in Jesus Christ, who became the substitute for our offenses. His love freely stands in your place of judgment ... if you want it. Otherwise, you get to stand before God and defend your righteousness and perfection based on your lifetime of thoughts, intentions, attitudes, and behaviors.

Because Jesus was God made into the likeness of man, His sacrifice was perfect, acceptable, and complete. Through suffering and dying on the cross, He effectively took upon Himself our judgment of eternal death and presents us pure and blameless before our Father God. In a holy transfer, Jesus substituted His blood payment for ours. Our response to that offering is our "second chance" of acceptance or rejection with the lover of our souls. Only this time, if we receive Christ's gift of redemption on our behalf, we also receive so much more.

Though our physical bodies still experience the natural realm, in the spirit realm, a divine deposit has been placed within those who gladly receive. It is Christ in us. Because of our union with Christ, He makes us coheirs of the kingdom of God where we can access the economy of heaven and the promises God outlines for us through His Word, the Bible. The laws of nature no longer define us. We are given access to a new identity, a new authority, a new power, and a new destiny. Of this new identity, we can say:

I AM redeemed (1 Peter 1:18–19).

I AM a new creation (2 Corinthians 5:17).

I AM born again (John 3:3–7).

I AM loved by God (1 John 4:10).
I AM salt and light in the world (Matthew 5:13–14).
I AM a temple of the Holy Spirit (1 Corinthians 6:19).
I AM God's son or daughter (Romans 8:14).
I AM justified and glorified (Romans 8:30).
I AM healed (Isaiah 53:5).

And of this new authority, we can say:
I AM a coheir with Christ (Romans 8:17).
I AM a friend of Jesus (John 15:15).
I AM a saint (Romans 1:7).
I AM part of a royal priesthood (1 Peter 2:9).
I AM Christ's ambassador (2 Corinthians 5:20).
I AM a child of God (1 John 3:1–2).
I AM part of the body of Christ (1 Corinthians 12:27).

And of this new power we have received, we can say:
I have been given the Spirit of sonship (Romans 8:15).
I have the Spirit of God, which lives in me (1 John 3:24).
I have the fullness of the Deity inside me (Colossians 2:9–10).
I have rivers of living water flowing through and from me (John 7:38).
I have the light of life (John 8:12).
I have the keys to the kingdom (Matthew 16:9).
I have incomparably great power like that which raised Christ from the dead (Ephesians 1:18–21).
I AM enriched in every way; in all my speaking and knowledge (1 Corinthians 1:5–7).
I AM a partaker of His divine nature (2 Peter 1:3–4).
I have power when the Holy Spirit comes on me (Acts 1:8).

I have a spirit of power, of love, and of self-discipline
(2 Timothy 1:7).
I have the full measure of God, His power at work
within me (Ephesians 3:16, 19–20).
I AM increasingly conforming to the likeness of his
son (Romans 8:29).
I have power to be more than a conqueror (Romans
8:37).
I have Christ's peace that is beyond understanding
that guards my heart and mind (John 14:27;
Philippians 4:7).

We have both the permission and position to live in a relationship with God we could never have attained for ourselves. Our identity is too corrupted by our willful participation with pride, ego, distrust, selfishness, self-sufficiency, and limited thinking. But when we exchange our corruptible nature for Christ's incorruptible Spirit, we become a new creation, even as we continue to live out our days in the natural world.

Human beings think negative thoughts. It is our nature. However, as we assimilate these truths into our thinking instead of the deficits upon which we tend to fixate, then to see ourselves as anything but lovely, holy, redeemed, healed, and equipped is to align ourselves with a lie. To live from certain faith not just cognitive belief in these spiritual truths makes it possible to be more than a conqueror over life's challenges, including disease. If I am a temple of God's Holy Spirit, and I have living water flowing from me, how can cancer, addiction, depression, and the like also live in me and survive? They cannot!

We can affirm these promises of God but not because we're good or have attained some spiritual superiority. When we actively receive God's gift of redemption through Jesus Christ, we put on His identity in the spirit realm, and God sees in us the reflection and image of His Son. We are given the outrageous opportunity to live as sons and daughters of the King in a heavenly inheritance that is more than a future theological position. It's a very real, viable experience with which to align our identity, our thinking, and our bodies now with who we are in Christ as defined by the Word of God given to us in Scripture. We have access and permission to declare what God's Word reveals about us, regardless of our circumstances or emotions. Limited, life-threatening thinking has no power to possess us except the control we give it.

We live in God and from God when we live in and from our heavenly potential. That's where we declare our true identity and receive our immediate and eternal inheritance. When we declare the truths of I AM, we are affirming or agreeing with God about who we really are through His eyes. It's neither wishful, positive thinking nor charismatic religion. It's the divine nature within us that gives us permission to think, be, and have more. And our agreement empowers faith to take root in our hearts and live on Earth as it is in heaven. It is here where the Spirit of transformation occurs, where the Word of God and the responsibility of the human heart intersect. It accomplishes a renewal of the mind and a restoration of the body.

Taming the Tongue

What's important to consider here, whether or not you accept this position in faith, is you're constantly affirming statements of "I am" as you believe them to be. But not all those "I am's" are redeeming, healthy, and aligned with life-giving truth. For example, think of all the ways you may have defined yourself in the last forty-eight hours. "I am sick; I have cancer; I'm no good at_____; I can't_____; I'm afraid of_____; I hate_____," etc.

In fact, from the fifty to sixty thousand thoughts per day that scientists estimate generate through your mind, the majority are negative or limiting and go unchecked. That's why the apostle Paul was so emphatic to take every thought captive and make it obedient unto Christ (2 Corinthians 10:5). Elsewhere, Scriptures tell us:

> "All kinds of animals, birds, reptiles, and creatures of the sea are being tamed and have been tamed by man, but no man can tame the tongue. It is a restless evil, full of deadly poison" (James 3:7–8).

> "Do not let any unwholesome talk come out of your mouths but only what is helpful for building others up according to their needs" (Ephesians 4:29).

> "Whoever of you loves life and desires to see many good days, keep your tongue from evil and your lips from speaking lies" (Psalm 34:12–13).

> "Whatever is true, noble, right, pure, lovely, admirable; if anything is excellent or praiseworthy—think about such things" (Philippians 4:8).

> "For whoever would love life and see good days must keep his tongue from evil and his lips from deceitful speech" (1 Peter 3:10).

> "The tongue has the power of life and death, and those who love it will eat its fruit" (Proverbs 18:21).

> "Do everything without complaining and arguing, so that you may become blameless and pure children of God" (Philippians 2:14–15).

These are not just mandates for the religious. God's Word always has practical application for our lives whether or not we claim to be His. The seeds of our thoughts, nurtured by what we say, always produce a harvest after their own kind. Unexamined, subconscious thinking and careless speech has physiological and psychological implications, influencing our very destiny. Our words create and reinforce our reality.

When we think—either in our minds or out loud—our thoughts are made up of three components: *words*, which give us *pictures* that elicit *emotions*. These three dimensions constitute what psychologists refer to as "self-talk." Self-talk can be expressed aloud or held quietly as the internal conversation you have with yourself. Individuals have self-talk; families have self-talk; organizations have self-talk; and even nations have self-talk. It's how we describe others, the world around us, and ourselves and is expressed in the following quotes:

> "Language is the dress of thought" (Samuel Johnson).
>
> "Every time we speak, our minds are on parade" (Unknown).
>
> "For out of the overflow of the heart the mouth speaks" (Matthew 12:34).

Throughout Scripture, the Word of God emphasizes the critical nature of self-talk. Why? Because our words and what we affirm produce energy that has the power to create life or death emotionally, physically, and spiritually, not only for ourselves but also in the lives of others. Our words are not lifeless expressions evaporating into thin air. We have all experienced how "reckless words pierce like a sword, but the tongue of the wise brings healing" (Proverbs 12:18), whether we've been the recipient or deliverer of such communication.

Beyond the psychological scarring of our self-image, negative, fear-based self-talk also creates a toxic environment within the body through the endocrine system. Dr. Caroline Leaf describes the anatomy of thought in her book, *Who Switched Off My Brain? Controlling Toxic Thoughts and Emotions*, where she describes how the primary gland of the endocrine system, the hypothalamus, has the job of responding to your thought life with the release of chemicals. The type of chemicals it releases is tied to your emotional state. Positive thoughts and feelings release helpful chemicals like feel-good endorphins and serotonin that boost your immune system, enhance memory, and help develop intelligence. Negative, fear-based thoughts release harmful chemicals like cortisol that causes inflammation, one of the major factors found in most chronic diseases. What scientists are finding more and more in the mind/body connection is these molecular chemicals attach to and actually change us on the cellular level. The way we think has everything to do with our immune system and DNA. Toxic thinking, i.e., anxiety, fear, depression, worry, hate, frustration, impatience, bitterness, etc., actually creates a deadly environment and over time changes our cells' makeup on the outside and the DNA on the inside. That's why it's all the more critical you control your emotions of fear and worry during times of chronic illness where your immune system is already in a compromised state. If you don't manage the way you think and speak about your life, it will eventually manage you.

This principle has just as much application in the organization as it does in the individual. The awareness of self-talk has been the single-most important concept impacting my work with corporations across the country. I have seen entire companies change their culture and bottom-line profitability as a result of discovering ways they were speaking themselves into their own roadblocks.

One large company is one of the top four trucking firms in the nation. In their driver-training schools, they routinely reinforced expectations and procedures to the new recruits. Unaware of how the mind works and the impact of coaching backward—giving people the picture of what you *don't* want—they communicated levels of performance, by neglect, that had become their "normal," "Within the first thirty days, you *will* have an accident."

That was their standard, and I suppose they thought emphasizing the inevitable would de-escalate driver anxiety. What they didn't realize was they were actually developing the mind-set and self-talk of their drivers with mental pictures of accidents, which stimulated anxiety and worry. To the extent these new drivers reinforced those images each time they got into their cabs, the release of fear-based chemicals actually impaired their judgment. The more they focused on what they didn't want through repetition of thought, the stronger the image of crashing became in their minds. It naturally became a self-fulfilling prophecy because we always move toward what we think about. They were unconsciously and subconsciously programming the company's accident rates into the minds of their new recruits by coaching their people toward the image of what they didn't want.

Once they figured this out and changed the way they trained, they saw an immediate return on their investment. For the first time in the company's history, they had three operating centers that reported no accidents in over sixty days. One center even reported a ninety-day, accident-free status. The financial impact on insurance and assets alone offset the cost of our consulting many times over. The measurable change in performance opened the door for us to expand our culture work deep throughout the larger organization and its international offices.

Often in our earnest to be "realistic" or to simply share with others the update of our current circumstances, we inadvertently keep ourselves ensnared by the images we reinforce. We pray for one thing but say another. And, of course, it's the words we speak that illuminate which reality is most dominant in our mind.

Being immersed in this information, I was particularly careful with my own self-talk during my diagnosis, treatment, and ongoing care. I knew how critical it was to constantly reinforce my image of wellness rather than the diagnosis of cancer. In order to create the mind-set that this was a short-term, momentary roadblock, I was intentional with my responses to others and never let myself say, "*my* cancer" or "I *have* cancer." Instead, I purposefully stated—and even do to this day—"I have been/was *diagnosed* with cancer."

While this may sound like insignificant semantics, I am emphatic not to align myself with a disease that doesn't have the right to inhabit my body. How often I hear people belly-up to their symptoms and continue to discuss their plight instead of focusing on the end result of healing. I refused to speak possessively of my circumstances, careful to keep it at arm's length rather than something to define me. To that end, I am quite careful about support groups spending too much time letting people identify with the disease and dwell on their present circumstances without giving them tools to focus on a worry-free, faith-filled mind-set. While there may be comfort in shared misery, the goal of healing is to focus on where you want to go, not on where you're currently stuck.

Another practical step I used to limit the negative self-talk yet keep loving friends and family updated was to start a blog. It was a critical tool to keep others informed of my journey while minimizing the continual repetition of facts and feelings that could too easily cause a downward spiral of fear, anxiety, and hopelessness. The discipline of finding choice words to express and release my emotions in brief updates was particularly cathartic.

If technology is not your friend, there are plenty of free sites established specifically to let you communicate to your select group of loved ones. CaringBridge.org is one of the most reputable sites to protect your privacy, yet it allows you to post and receive correspondence. If writing is not practical or preferable, find someone who will serve as the point person for communicating your journey to others. The last thing you need to do is continue to reinforce your current status with every well-wisher.

My mother has been my lifelong best friend. We are effortlessly open, non-withholding, and willing to do just about anything for one another. We have walked through deep and painful trials together, and she gave me every available resource she could to meet my time of need. When the second diagnosis of "incurable" cancer came, she was naturally devastated. She had already lost one child in her lifetime—something no mother or father should ever have to bear. For the first several months, she was overtly consumed with my fate. Her eyes teared up with deep sadness every time she greeted me. I felt like she looked at me and saw the grave, while I kept trying to visualize God's word in Jeremiah 29:11, " 'For I know the plans I have for you,' says the LORD. 'Plans to prosper you and not to harm you, plans to give you a hope and a future.' "

My mother talked incessantly about doctor appointments, prognoses, next steps, and "what if's." I realized this was her way of venting her worry and trying to establish some sense of control over the situation, and I tried to give her that space while buffering my own mental defenses. But I soon had to ask her to stop. I couldn't keep rehashing and reinforcing my own current reality. I needed to surround myself with people who would look at me with positive expectancy and talk about God's healing. I asked her to rest on my certain faith until she could develop the belief of her own. And she did! In fact, once she grasped my perspective and the wisdom of speaking about life, she became my biggest cheerleader.

In the same way, you must guard yourself from well-meaning people who want to commiserate with you in your present circumstances rather than your inherited potential. Search out support and surround yourself with people who bring light and laughter and vision into your environment. Brainstorm, dream, and describe things you see yourself doing six months, one year, and three years from now. Write them down and talk to others about them. Keep a close watch on how you speak about your situation. Reject possessive words like *my* or *I have* when it comes to discussing your medical condition. Meditate on the Word of God so you know His truths and are able to declare what He says about you after you've just walked out the doctor's office. Become conscious of your subconscious thinking patterns, taking every thought captive and making sure it reflects God's life-giving reality. Your self-talk will reveal your mind-set, whether you dwell on the diagnosis of disease or talk about your faith-filled future. And you eventually move toward the most dominant ideas you think and express.

Reflection Activity

1. Make a list with two columns. At the top of each, write the heading, "I Am." Under the first column, list all the adjectives that describe characteristics about yourself that you like. Under the second column, list characteristics about yourself that are neutral, negative, or you would like to change.
2. Review your lists. Is one longer than the other? Was one quicker or easier to make than the other?

3. As you reread the words or phrases, whose voice do you hear speaking? Your parents? A coach? Your spouse? Circle the ones that are in full alignment with the truth of your identity in God. Create new "I Am" statements for the ones that you want to change.

4. Do you have a clear vision of your future beyond your current diagnosis? If not, why not? If so, what does it look like? Be specific. Write it down. Then share it with someone you trust.

5. Do you have your own personal support group of individuals who are speaking hope and vision and healing into your life? If so, who are they? If not, begin *now* to build your own healing coalition of supporters. Seek out others who have experienced healing to be a help to you. Make a conscious effort to spend scheduled time in conversation with them so they can help you stay on track with your thoughts, words, activities, and spiritual beliefs.

Picture Perfect:
Creating Health and Wellness
in the Midst of Disease

Blog Entry: June 30, 2009

Standing Firm

THERE'S NOTHING LIKE PERSISTENT DISCOMFORT to tear down even the most steadfast spirit. It's certainly easier to have a sure faith and positive outlook when you are feeling just fine. But the last several weeks have shown me how physical weariness can gnaw away at you, trying to rob you of your joy, peace, and certainty.

I've been eating all the right foods and taking plenty of supplements, but my immune system doesn't seem to be doing the job of warding off illness. In the past five weeks, I've had three bouts of bacterial and flu symptoms.

It's no small coincidence this present one—now in day eleven—nabbed me just three days after attending a healing service. The Tuesday evening service is a ministry of a church across town where the pastor spent six months hospitalized for a rare blood cancer. In his book, Hope Beyond Reason, Dave Hess recounts his miraculous healing and God's calling on him to provide a healing ministry to the community. Many documented healings have occurred there, and friends encouraged me to check it out.

This wasn't some souped-up, charismatic road show. The atmosphere was quiet and reflective; the worship music was melodic and free-form. Brent, along with my prayer buddies Cathy and Teresa, came to support me, and we each had this overwhelming sense of the presence of God the minute we entered the sanctuary.

I hadn't felt anything like that in quite some time. The love and tenderness of God was so evident I was overcome with tears, not from self-pity but from sensing God's lavish love over me. I left with a heartfelt belief that God was healing the cancer metastases on my spine.

By Friday, I received a cryptic text message from my business partner Steve. He warned me about not giving into false symptoms designed to cause fear and doubt in my mind. He differentiated instantaneous miracles from healing—an abiding by faith in the knowledge that I have received God's promises found in Scripture. I wasn't quite sure why he was sending this to me. It was a gorgeous Friday afternoon, and I was at the pool with Nicholas, feeling perfectly whole. I texted him back, thanking him for the message. Little did I know how prophetic his words would be.

The next day I awoke feeling achy and finding it uncomfortable to swallow. As Nic's swim meet wore on, I wore down. By evening, Brent and I were sitting at a wedding reception where I felt so horrible I couldn't eat, so we left early. The body aches lasted several days, and my throat was sore too. I couldn't get off the couch and missed the first three nights of Nicholas' Vacation Bible School. On Friday, pink eye plagued me, getting deeper and darker as the weekend wore on. I sported sunglasses everywhere I went, knowing just the sight of me would cause others to go into contagious frenzy. By last night, with body aches and sore glands starting all over again, I thought about how weary it must be for people who live with chronic pain.

Through this whole cancer saga, I have been asymptomatic. Because of that, three oncologists, my surgeon, and the radiologist/oncologist all advise to wait before doing any additional treatment. Currently, I am on hormone therapy, taking a tiny pill once a day. Though they are drawing blood on a monthly basis to check my cancer markers, I won't be scanned again until mid-August to see if this form of therapy is working. It's been easy to stay encouraged when I don't feel badly. No heroism in that. But I see it takes greater conviction of mind and spirit to keep your joy when the physical wants to convince you that you're weak and losing the fight.

Circumstances can test faith or build perseverance—it all depends on what picture is more dominant in the mind: the picture of healing, or my fleeting circumstances. I stand firm on healing, and let circumstances be what they may.

Healing hugs,
Doreen

Choose Release:
Resolving the Wounds that Kill Us

IN ANY AREA OF YOUR life where you have not been living in the fullness of who God intended you to be, the steps of realization and reflection will ultimately reveal limiting beliefs that you have been operating in on a subconscious level that have been holding you back. As you discover the root of where these ideas first developed, you will often find they belong to voices outside yourself as the opinions of others you allowed to haphazardly shape your identity along the path of life. In other cases, the voice may be an internal one where you once made a vivid proclamation in protective response to a painful situation. And though it may have been a statement of survival at that moment, it's trapping you from moving forward into particular areas of your life. Both voices not only restrict the truth of your potential, but they often carry the weight of negative emotions embedded in your memory, subconsciously justifying why you act and behave as you do.

For example, the excruciating pain of my parents' divorce and the long-term consequences it had on our family made me swear, "I will *never* get divorced!" That may seem like a reasonable and noble stance in today's superficial society where we jump in and out of marriages because "it no longer makes me happy." But what I didn't realize until I was into my mid-thirties was this pain-laden vow caused me to subconsciously push away many wonderful men who had come into my life. My dating relationships were mainly loving, monogamous, and long-term. But ultimately each fell apart, along with the accusations my expectations were too high or I was too demanding. While it was painful to examine my heart and see myself as anything but loving and devoted, I discovered a profound truth impacting my deepest desires. The very things I longed for— committed love, protection, and faithfulness—were the very things I was subconsciously sabotaging by my fear of abandonment and rejection. Though I had an intellectual understanding of how my dad's decisions had impacted me, I hadn't resolved the fear-based triggers that continued to manifest in anger, criticism, and judgment toward others and myself.

The process of revelation shows us the root of these emotion-packed memories and the pain, fear, and anger associated with them. These emotions are not one-time occurrences tucked neatly away in the recesses of our mind. Every time we encounter situations that mirror or even remotely resemble those memories on the subconscious level, our minds automatically retrieve and release the emotional state associated with it, both chemically and behaviorally. To the extent we dismiss and permit these restricting beliefs and toxic emotions to dominate our decisions going forward, we live in bondage to our histories and inhibit the fullness and freedom we were meant to live in Christ. Our fears keep us in darkness and block us from experiencing the goodness of God and His loving intimacy. Moreover, these negative emotions continue to build up toxic chemicals in our bodies that eventually exhibit themselves as disease. Until we resolve and release that which was stolen from us, we continue to bleed spiritually and emotionally and manifest the results in our health and lack of well-being.

It is naturally instinctive for us to dress the areas of injury we've experienced with justifications, habits, and attitudes to shield us from further attack. These reactions to pain are subconscious defense mechanisms. We retract and withhold, or we lash out and exact revenge. When we consciously prod our pain or derive a sense of identity from it, we run the risk of parading it around with pride, self-righteousness, and judgment. This takes on a victimized mentality of terminal uniqueness—"Well, you don't know *my* story"—where we live in a state of hypersensitivity and stress. Whether we attribute the source of our pain to God, others, or ourselves, the remedy is to heal our wounds. We must stop burying them under layers of fear and denial or feeding them with anger, ambivalence, worry, sorrow, bitterness, or hate. It takes a supernatural act of vulnerability and resolution. It takes the balm of forgiveness—the root of all healing.

Forgiveness is not a feeling. It doesn't require that you sense safety or renewed relationship or emotions of trust and pleasure with the perpetrator of your heart. It doesn't demand that you tolerate injustice or continue to expose yourself to harmful situations. Forgiveness is an act of the will, and it has tremendous power to destroy strongholds in both the natural and spirit realms. It acknowledges pain and impropriety but determines not to live under the crushing weight of fear or captivity to harmful emotions. It gives up the need to be right, repaid, recognized, or respected. Forgiveness releases a change of perspective where we claim an internal locus of control rather than remain enslaved by outside circumstances. We consciously decide to live free from corrosive impulses and emotions so future FEAR (False Evidence Appearing Real) does not gain a foothold and strangle the light and life we were meant to live.

No matter how deep you've drawn the lines in the sand or how justified you feel for the wrongs enacted against you, how convinced you are past injuries no longer hurt, or how raw and vivid your pain might currently be, God is in the business of redemption and renewal. He always seeks to save and restore. That is His nature. His heavenly grace is a salve sufficient to heal the areas of hurt you are willing to offer up to Him.

Forgiveness is a gift to receive but also a command to follow. The New Testament is quite clear—the measure of our forgiveness from God is proportional to the measure of forgiveness we extend to others. It is through the natural eye that we are judicious in seeking retribution and condemnation on others. When we gaze with spiritual eyes on what it cost God to forgive our own debt, we can hardly hold others hostage to their misconducts. Instead, our joy and gratitude naturally level the playing field. If we expect mercy for ourselves, we must offer it to others in kind.

"Our Father ... Forgive us our debts as we have forgiven our debtors" (Matthew 6:9, 12).

"And when you stand praying, if you hold anything against anyone, forgive him so that your Father in heaven may forgive you your sins" (Mark 11:25).

"Therefore, if you are offering your gift at the altar and there remember that your brother has something against you, leave your gift there in front of the altar. First go and be reconciled to your brother; then come and offer your gift" (Matthew 5:23–24).

"For if you forgive men when they sin against you, your heavenly Father will also forgive you. But if you do not forgive men their sins, your Father will not forgive your sins" (Matthew 6:14–15).

"Peter came to Jesus and asked, 'Lord, how many times shall I forgive my brother when he sins against me? Up to seven times?' Jesus answered, 'I tell you not seven times, but seventy-seven times' " (Matthew 18:21–22).

"Be kind and compassionate to one another, forgiving each other, just as in Christ God forgave you" (Ephesians 4:32).

"Bear with each other and forgive any grievances you may have against one another. Forgive as the Lord forgave you" (Colossians 3:13).

All have sinned and fall short of the glory of God (Romans 3:23). There is not one of us who stands free from judgment, and yet "God did not send his Son into the world to condemn the world, but to save the world through him" (John 3:17). Even as Jesus hung in innocence, dying for our misdeeds, He asked the Father to "Forgive them, for they do not know what they are doing" (Luke 23:34). If Jesus Himself released forgiveness over us, how is it we play the role of judge and juror over others for lesser crimes? As His followers, we are to be ambassadors of Christ's message of forgiveness (2 Corinthians 5:20) and ministers of reconciliation in a caustic and hurting world (2 Corinthians 5:18).

Forgiveness takes the form of giving and receiving. You pursue forgiveness to resolve situations where you have been the offense to others, and you extend forgiveness to release those who formerly offended you. In some cases, you may be the subject of your own forgiveness. Poor decisions or regrettable actions you continue to harbor against yourself must be let go. If you have already asked God for forgiveness, you can be assured He is faithful and just and will remove your offenses as far as the east is from the west (1 John 1:9; Psalm 103:12). Any further condemnation you hear comes from the pit of hell not from the Spirit of God. Because satan (lowercase *s* is by design; he doesn't deserve a capital *s*) is a liar and always speaks his native tongue, his ploy is to remind us of our emotional baggage and undermine our confidence in who we are in Christ. Jesus, on the other hand, came to set the captives free. If you have confessed your sins and your need for a savior, you are free indeed! Your conscience can be cleansed and your memories healed. It's time to open your hands and heart in release so you might receive grace and make peace with your soul. "I forgive myself and others for all the wrongs done to me, and I take responsibility for my own life" is a powerful and liberating affirmation of healing forgiveness to live by.

In other cases, you may have felt angry toward God for situations you attributed to His doing. The loss of loved ones, personal safety, resources, or opportunities for health and happiness—those unexplainable sufferings—can sometimes be a source of scorn toward God. Often when we can't explain the "why" of hurtful circumstances, we wrongly reduce God to the level of our experiences. We make erroneous assumptions when we equate every outcome in life with the will of God. And we malign His character when we attribute sin, sickness, temptation, violence, or vengeance to His nature. If you have blamed God for being unkind, unfair, unloving, or unjust, bring those open wounds to Him in prayer. He desires to heal you and set you free from bitterness, apathy, and powerlessness.

Perhaps you were raised with the wrong impression of God as a mean, avenging taskmaster, always spying to see if you are naughty or nice. Even our past religious conditioning may have caused us to feel God is always angry with us, tallying up the score of all our wrongdoings. Or perhaps you equate God's character with those of individuals who stood in authority over you. For instance, if your natural father was absent, abusive, or inattentive, you may have subconsciously attributed those characteristics toward God. But He already knows your every thought. You don't have to hide in shame, guilt, anger, or embarrassment. Simply confess where you blame Him for feeling cheated, that life was unfair, or where you felt entitled to different outcomes. The book of Psalms is a perfect example of how God's people cried out to Him in a myriad of emotions, i.e., sorrow, fear, frustration, abandonment, weariness, and revenge, and yet they always returned to acknowledging His ways as higher than theirs. If you've distanced yourself from the love and healing God desires to pour out over you, simply tell Him you're sorry for how you've kept Him out of your life. His desire for you is to make all things new.

The act of forgiving is sometimes like unpeeling an onion, where God's Spirit will reveal to our spirit deeper layers of protective, limited thinking we've built up over time to hide the core of our vulnerable heart. In other words, we sometimes don't get it done all at once. While we can be assured forgiveness in the spirit realm takes place the minute we ask it of God, in the natural, our beliefs and behaviors may still be colored with the residue of pain. We don't necessarily feel it when we're sitting in a safe and comfortable environment. But when we are confronted with similar challenges or feeling out of our comfort zone, those automatic, reactive tendencies reveal we're still operating from fear or anger-filled, limiting beliefs. Until we uproot and replace old defensive patterns, we are still keeping them alive. Conscious control can only suppress them. To experience healing, we must extract and exchange them. The deeper the hurt we've experienced, and the more we've reinforced beliefs and emotions to protect us over the years, the more layers we likely have to peel away.

Whether we forgive out of obedience to God, from grateful recognition of His mercy over our own lives, or as the basis from which healing occurs, the objective of this inner process is the gift of peace. Peace and contentment are Spirit-driven qualities that quiet our mind and body. They often elude us in many areas of our lives because we go after them the wrong way. We look for them in the things of this world, when we were created to find them in an intimate relationship with God. There is nothing He created in heaven or on Earth that will give us more peace and pleasure than God Himself. It is His design for the human heart that only He can fill.

Jesus understood this yearning that our souls seek. That was his purpose. "He was pierced for our transgressions, he was crushed for our iniquities; the punishment that brought us *peace* was upon him, and by his wounds we are healed" (Isaiah 53:5, emphasis mine). In all ways, Jesus purchased our peace and wholeness. He heals us spiritually from our sins; He heals us emotionally with His peace; and by His wounds our illnesses and diseases are healed. Peace becomes the product of reconciliation we access through His death and resurrection. "Peace I leave with you; my peace I give you. I do not give to you as the world gives. Do not let your hearts be troubled and do not be afraid" (John 14:27).

Where we don't experience the peace Christ Jesus offers us are those places where we are not willing to let go of the past. Some people love to live in the past. It's their distinctiveness, their fuel for emotional energy, and their platform for attention. They prefer the pattern of martyr, always living in a state of crisis and excuses. I've seen families, organizations, entire communities, and whole races of people define themselves by what has been rather than grow into a vision of newness. When we stay entrenched in the past, we have no vision for the future. And "where there is no vision, the people perish" (Proverbs 29:18 KJV).

Resolving and releasing the wounds of your past and present is your opportunity to forget what is behind and to strain toward what is ahead, that you may "press on toward the goal to win the prize for which God has called [you] heavenward in Christ Jesus" (Philippians 3:13). It is an internal process of forgiveness and a healing of memories that purifies your spirit and activates an environment for wholeness. It allows the light of God's love and truth to expose areas of darkness where satan has capitalized on hurtful circumstances and kept you chained to your past. It is a sanctifying process that breaks spiritual, emotional, and physical strongholds over you and allows new life to breed health and healing.

Reflection Activity

1. Take twenty-thirty minutes of quiet reflection. Put yourself in an environment where you can close your eyes and picture your past. Ask the Holy Spirit to take you back to your earliest remembrances of infancy deeply embedded in your memory. Let the Spirit bring images of your family members and caregivers to mind. As you recall interactions, family gatherings, holidays, and activities, ask the Holy Spirit to illuminate occurrences where love and acceptance where not there for you (either by intent or neglect). Ask Jesus to replace those old painful memories with His unconditional love and value for you. Out loud and by name, release the responsible individuals to God. Declare, "God, I forgive (the person's name) from (name the occurrence) and

replace the pain trigger of (name the emotion) with Your love and peace that passes all understanding. Thank You, Jesus, for Your sacrifice that has brought my healing."

After you and the Holy Spirit have removed all fears established in your childhood, move to your early school years. Think of teachers, coaches, schoolmates, neighbors, pastors, or clergy who may have embarrassed, betrayed, or humiliated you. In the same process, confess your forgiveness and release of each person. Be sure to ask Jesus to resolve your painful emotions and thank Him for the indwelling of His love and grace over each infringement.

Repeat this process for your teen years of junior and senior high school, asking Jesus to heal memories of hurt, guilt, failure, and fear.

Next, go into your adult years of college and/or work and/or marriage. Recall areas of disappointment, humiliation, and pain from professors, employers, dating relationships, spouses, and in-laws. Think of your children who have hurt you. Think of situations where you felt guilty or inadequate as a parent. Ask Jesus to set you free from every painful memory.

For circumstances of death, illness, injury, and financial hardship, ask Jesus to remove the heavy weight of anger, grief, fear, and depression. Ask Him to renew your joy and fill you in every area or circumstance that robbed you of His light and life and love. Thank Him for His amazing love and delight over you, for giving all of Himself to make you whole. Thank Him for His peace that passes all understanding and that guards your heart and mind. Praise Him for His glory, honor, and power.

2. Now that you have resolved and released old pain triggers caused by others, repeat this process by examining your own life and the places where you caused pain to others. As memories emerge along your chronological life, ask God to forgive you for the offense and ask that He replace the emotions of anger, shame, embarrassment, retaliation, fear, and failure that have corrupted your mind. As you forgive yourself, resolve these memories, and release the emotions, be sure to fill the void with Jesus' love, light, and life.

3. Finally, think through your life again and recall the places where you felt hurt by God. Recall circumstances where you felt life was unfair, you were cheated, or you felt unloved. Recall times where you thought your prayers went unanswered, God was absent or unkind, or things didn't turn out the way you wanted. Confess to Him the ways in which you gave up on Him, intentionally distanced yourself from Him, or rebelled by trying to fill your spirit with all kinds of things this world can't satisfy. As memories surface, ask forgiveness for how you wrongly maligned God's character, didn't give Him the reverence and respect due His glory, and harbored negative emotions against Him. Thank Him for His mercy, His unfathomable gift of salvation, His desire for your restoration, and His Spirit of power within you.

Picture Perfect:
Creating Health and Wellness in the Midst of Disease

Blog Entry: July, 2009

Growing Gardens

I SPENT THE MORNING WEEDING AGAIN, which was probably not the greatest activity for my back. But it's useless. I just can't help myself. The minute I see those menacing greens sprouting through my mulch, I get completely obsessed. For some unfathomable reason, I take it as a personal affront they are back again after my last backbreaking episode of digging and spraying. I hold this unrealistic expectation that one valiant extraction for the season is all it should take to keep my grounds pruned and pristine for the summer. If I had known the constant attention required to keep weeds from populating my plants, I would have zero-scaped our yard or filled it in with rocks.

In the midst of these musings, it quickly occurred to me my mind is much like my garden. The seeds I plant there produce after their kind. And though I desire and even envision breathtaking landscapes of health and happiness, it requires constant attention to keep the weeds of doubt, fear, suspicion, and resignation away. Though it would be so much easier to make a sporadic affirmation of faith in my wellness and pull out any negativity that has grown, I realize that by the time those weeds appear on the surface they have already been taking root in my heart. A pain here, a persistent cough there, an ache in my back I'm certain is well below the muscle and deep in the spine—those little physiological occurrences, prior to my diagnosis, would have been easily dismissed. Now they get sifted through this filter of fear called "cancer."

I know it's not just me. It's a universal principle applied to all humankind and has been explained across the ages. In the language of the mind, it's described as "teleological"—we move toward what we think about. In the language of the heart, the Apostle Paul implored us to "hold every thought captive unto Christ." Why? Because, "Whatsoever a man sows, that also shall he reap" (Galatians 6:7). In the halls of science, it is known as the biology of belief. Popularized by Dr. Bruce Lipton, our DNA does not control our biology; our DNA is controlled by signals received from outside the cells, including energy from positive and negative thoughts. Regardless of our bent, we are endowed with creative power born from the thoughts we nourish and fertilized by what we say.

So here I am in this season of stagnation, waiting for my next PET CT on August 26. I'm disappointed that the longer and deeper I've gotten into all of this, the less vigilant I've been about guarding my thoughts and words. I found myself challenged this week in conversation with a friend who doesn't understand my trust in God's promises and my body's ability to heal. The blades of her comments struck close to the root of my beliefs. "But you were into all of this faith and wellness stuff before, and look, it just came right back." What if she's right? What if this is pure folly? Are those backaches really the cancer growing? What will people say of me and my God if the scans aren't good? Seeds of doubt and fear eroding my landscape of peace. We move toward what we think about.

Grace like rain arrived the next day in the form of a forwarded e-mail from my friend Mike. Written by Rick Warren, author of *The Purpose Driven Life*, this message reminded me that faith grows not in ease and comfort but when we get to use it or test it when we are challenged by waiting, roadblocks, or thwarted expectations. Then choice factors in: resilience or resignation; determination or doubt; trust or temptation. " 'According to your faith, it will be done for you,' Jesus said" (Matthew 9:29). Well, if my beliefs determine my future, I want a big faith with a growing garden of expectations only God can fill. That may require more testing before triumph, but "everything is possible for him who believes" (Mark 9:23).

Healing hugs,
Doreen

Choose Joy:
Expanding the Attitude of Gratitude

IT WAS A YEAR AFTER my youngest brother had been killed in a car accident, and I was grappling with life, death, and grief. I was back in college, finishing my undergraduate degree after a seven-year tenure of international modeling in New York, Hamburg, Paris, Tokyo, and Washington DC. Distressed with the loss of my brother, I took an elective class on "Aging and the Aged" and was required to do a research paper. My hypothesis stated that when people have the opportunity and privilege to approach death, they naturally move toward the things of God. In other words, their hearts soften as they eagerly anticipate heaven.

My research consisted of interviewing elderly residents of a local home for the aging. The interviews were random, set up in advance by the administrators of the facility. I came in on a Saturday armed with questions about life experiences, future hopes, and expectations of life after death. The participants' candor was impressive, but my theory was quickly crushed.

The first gentleman I interviewed was stout and messy. Years of disappointment were etched in the frowns and scowls of his skin. His eyes were dark and lifeless. Although he had been aware of and agreed to my topic in advance of my arrival, he snarled his responses as if the very idea of my inquiries were insulting to him. Perhaps he just needed to vent. His demeanor stunned and intimidated me as I continued my line of questioning.

Though his story didn't sound remarkably unique, he revealed a life journey filled with frustration and disappointment. Alone in this world, he had outlived his wife and peers. He felt cheated by life but never divulged dreams that had been dashed. He was tired and spiritless and held no vision for life beyond death. God had abandoned him long ago, so he abandoned any hope of heaven. When you die, you die. That's that, and that was fine with him.

I sat glum and deflated as I waited for my next interviewee and wondered how I would now re-craft my research paper. Anger rose within me as I thought about this man who, in contrast to my brother's quick and violent death, had his whole life to prepare his heart and mind for heaven. He had nothing but opportunity in front of him to harness the power of perspective and live out his days in Spirit-filled destiny rather than pessimistic defeat. I was jarred by the reality of choices and consequences—how someone in his condition could look God in the face and say no.

I would have all but abandoned my topic if it had not been for what followed. My next interviewee was an elderly woman in her nineties. A facility staff person wheeled her to our quiet corner in the Social Room. Her smile was so youthful and infectious, I giggled as she approached. A petite, frail woman, she was perfectly coiffed. She wore a crisp dress with thick hose and heavy orthopedic shoes overpowering her skeletal legs. A pearl necklace graced her neck with matching earrings hanging precariously from sagging lobes. Delicate white gloves accented her tiny wrists. She was a radiant sight, drawing attention and smiles from everyone around her. I wasn't sure if this was her usual demeanor or if she made a special appearance for our day. It was too inappropriate to ask, and I felt a bit embarrassed by the insignificance of my school paper compared to the efforts she likely made to be so wonderfully presentable.

I sat mesmerized as her life story unfolded like a novel. As a young child, she and her sister moved to China where her parents were missionaries preaching the gospel of Christ. She recounted a happy, loving, close-knit family with deep respect and admiration for her parents. Then in the dark of night, she and her sister were severed from their mother and father. As a Communist China became more restrictive and antagonistic toward religious thinking, their lives became more endangered. Military began raiding towns and villages trying to eradicate the new regime of dangerous proselytizers. Knowing their imminent demise, her parents had the girls smuggled out of their village in the middle of the night, hiding them in large handwoven baskets until they crossed the border into the safety of waiting caregivers. As for her parents … well, she never heard from them again.

She we went on to describe the many blessings of her life. She spoke of her deceased husband with a blushing twinkle reminiscent of when they first met. She also talked lovingly and with great pride about her children, all who had died before her. Though her eyes transformed momentarily as she relived those darker moments of loss and suffering, she rebounded with such tenderness and appreciation for an abundant life well lived. Her joy exposed the negative veneer I had placed over my own life. And it jolted me that I more likely resembled the sour man of my first interview than this celebratory woman of faith. She held great anticipation for eternity with her loving Lord. And I made it my conscious prayer that day that I would grow old in the same beauty and grace this woman exuded so effortlessly. It was my first poignant lesson that gratitude isn't the product of a perfect life; gratitude is an attitude—a conscious, consistent choice we cultivate in life.

I wish I could say my conversion was complete that day. It was not. Yes, we were both women of faith, and we each shared experiences of deep loss and pain shaping our lives. But it was many more years before I grasped the concept of gratitude as something bigger and deeper than the learned behavior of a polite and gracious response. Gratitude is an overflowing from a joy-filled heart. But it is also a discipline we can develop. It reflects the attitude of our inner spirit—the direction in which we naturally lean as we come across the opportunities and challenges of life.

It is critical we become more diligent in observing and correcting the attitudes of our heart. Why? Proverbs 4:23 tells us, "Above all else, guard your heart, for it is the wellspring of life." Our heart is the fountainhead or origin of our well-being. We either align ourselves with a spirit of joyful thanksgiving that produces abundant fruit and keeps us alive or we bear bitterness, anxiety, and complaint from cultivating a spirit of scarcity and want. The lens we choose to develop will bring greater focus and clarity to what we dwell on. And the job of the Reticular Activating System is to allow your senses to pick up and filter information to your brain congruent with your outlook. Think lack, see lack, experience lack. Think abundance, see abundance, experience abundance.

I used to get up each morning and dwell on my to-do list. I felt burdened and weighed down until I could check off the line items of utmost importance. I held the belief that I couldn't relax until I finished everything I had to do. I put a tremendous load on myself. In fact, the heaviness manifested in my shoulders, where my neck and upper back were always tight and in constant pain.

For many years, developing a meaningful time of prayer and reflection in the mornings was difficult. It was hard to quiet my mind. I felt constantly overwhelmed with the have-to's of life, which made me angry, bitter, and jealous of those who seemed to have things so much easier. I kept thinking I was responsible for keeping everything tidy and under control, and I found it exhausting to be so strong all the time.

I naturally assumed it was because I was single for so long and had only myself to attend to all life's responsibilities. But even after I married at age thirty-six, I saw the same tendencies. In fact, they got worse, as I assumed Brent would eagerly apprehend all my have-to's with the same focus, priority, and attention I had given them. But he didn't. He was fun first and chores later. And I became even more frustrated, as I allowed an antagonistic attitude to overshadow my marriage.

The more I dwelled on what wasn't right, the more evidence I found to support it, reinforcing my negative beliefs about life, marriage, and Brent. It was a downward spiral that began a quick descent. And I realized I needed to make a choice: change my marriage or change my attitude. Thankfully, I decided to change my attitude.

I began to write down and affirm all the wonderful things about Brent and what he contributes to my life. His attributes and strengths *far* outweigh the differences in how we approach some things. As I revisited this list over and over, I began to see a change in the way I looked at him. More than that, God reminded me just how much He loves me by answering a long-held prayer. Because of my family and poor history with men, I always prayed God would protect me from marrying the wrong man. And He did. He knew Brent was just who I needed in my life.

As much as I needed an attitude fix with Brent, I needed a gratitude fix with God. I began to acknowledge and thank Him for the abundance of good things in my life. It's been many years now, but I can't imagine starting my day without my time of prayer, worship, and reflection. In fact, I'm not the same person when the pressures of time or schedule cause me to reposition it somewhere else in the day. You see, I established a new and more fruitful belief: "I am more effective and efficient when I begin my day in God's priorities rather than mine." As I meditate on the gift of life He's given me, healing in my body, the ability to move freely and effortlessly, and to have sight to read His Word and see the sun break into the morning sky, I am drawn to Him and His goodness and see a world of opportunity, blessing, and adventure He has prepared for me that is new every morning.

Gratitude is an outward expression of an inward condition where our focus is properly placed on God and His provision rather than on what's wrong, what's missing, and what's not happening. The joy in our heart manifests in the praise of our lips. "The good man brings good things out of the good stored up in his heart, and the evil man brings evil things out the evil stored up in his heart. For out of the overflow of his heart his mouth speaks" (Luke 6:45).

Though this has now become one of my daily affirmations, I remember asking God how someone is genuinely able to "Be joyful always; pray continually; give thanks in all circumstances, for this is God's will for you in Christ Jesus" (1 Thessalonians 5:16–18). In the midst of ravaging disease, painful death, or great devastation, how do we feel joy and express thanks for our sufferings with any degree of authenticity? Theologically, we're told to render our trials as all joy. When we contemplate Christ's sufferings—carrying the weight of all the world's sins over all of time—our circumstances look light in comparison. And yet the idea of rejoicing in suffering seems impossible, even ridiculous, as long as we continue to reside in our current reality.

Choosing joy is not about being synthetic in the heat of the battle. A mentor once told me, "It's okay to *get* afraid; it's not okay to *stay* afraid." Having the mind to heal is more than the absence of fear. It's the ability to apprehend your thinking and recognize false evidence appearing real before it takes root in your heart and permeates your spirit, your perspective, and your physical body. It's taking captive any negative self-talk before it begins a downward spiral, out of control. It's the spiritual wisdom and insight to reframe your worldly circumstances from a heavenly perspective. It shifts the loss of a loved one to thankfulness for his or her impact in your life, for the quality and quantity of time you shared together, and for the ways you became a better person as a result of his or her spirit touching yours.

Gratitude is a heart condition that, regardless of the circumstances, energetically looks for what's right and actively keeps alive defining moments where God's grace and power intervened in our circumstances of the past, both personally and historically. This exercise of remembering, affirming, and reinforcing God's good works enable us to disembowel anger and obliterate fear so self-focus, deficit, and dis-ease cannot take root and rob us of hope.

An active discipline of gratitude expands faith as you dwell on what's good and positive, and it creates expectancy for more. It trains us toward the art of receiving, which builds confidence and resiliency during times of challenge. "If God did it before, He can do it again. If He did it for her, He can do it for me." It creates our basis for trust, which begets deeper levels of peace that enables us to rest in the midst of the storm. "You will keep in perfect peace him whose mind is steadfast because he trusts in You" (Isaiah 26:3). As our spirit celebrates in the abundance of God's goodness and provision, our mind builds and looks for positive assurance and our brain releases life-producing chemicals to bring health and peace to our body.

Choosing joy transfers the attention from who we are to who God is so we are able to shift our circumstances from where we are to where God is. We do this through the posture of praise and worship that moves us into the presence of God. As we choose joy, praise, and rejoicing, presenting our requests to God through prayer with expectant thanksgiving, He gives us His supernatural peace to keep our hearts and minds safe and steadfast in Christ Jesus (Philippians 4:4–6).

Reflection Activity

1. Make a list of all the people, possessions, and opportunities, past, present, and future, for which you are grateful.

2. Spend time over the next few weeks reviewing your list. Beside each entry, write one word that best describes what each person, place, or thing has given you. Be intentional to find the most uniquely specific word to describe the impact you've felt or received.

3. In what areas or for which people in your life can you be more grateful?

4. Think of your present circumstances. Looking through the lens of gratitude, what things have you learned or

experienced about God, others, and yourself that you did not see or realize prior to now?

5. Select four to five people this week who have impacted you. Take the time to find creative ways to express to each of them the gratitude you feel for their impact on your life. If you really want to be an influence in the lives of others and leave a legacy to be remembered, make this a habit in your life. Be intentional to plan it out. Take three to four people each week from your list in Activity #1 and share how grateful you are for knowing them.

Picture Perfect:
Creating Health and Wellness in the Midst of Disease

Blog Entry: August, 2009

Heavenly Healing

WHAT IF YOU WERE TOLD the beliefs you hold determine how your life goes? Would it change the way you think about your circumstances? And what if you learned your self-talk either moves you closer to your hopes, goals, and prayers or it negates them? Would it cause you to take every thought captive and think before you speak? Or what if someone said that if you have faith, you can ask for anything, and as long as you don't have doubt in your heart, it will be accomplished? Could you trust, waiting patiently in the unseen while current reality stares you in the face? These are some of the opportunities I have lived in for the past seven months, which allowed me to move stronger and deeper into a commitment that says, "Okay, Jesus. You said all these things. So I am taking You at Your word and believing You with all my heart."

Perhaps it's the quality of the crisis confronting us that impacts our hope, faith, and trust. Let's face it, when you're diagnosed with stage four, "incurable" cancer that has gone into your bloodstream and begun to manifest itself in other areas of your body, there's not much to lose in looking like a religious zealot. In fact, even among nonbelievers, there is sympathetic license to talk and walk in ways that would otherwise be considered alienating or politically incorrect, at best.

Some have been dumbfounded by my "cavalier" attitude toward the medical professionals involved in my case. It's not that I've been disregarding their diagnoses or protocols; I just don't put my focus, faith, hope, and life in their hands. They're certainly a vehicle for restoring health and wholeness, but so are the nutrients and exercise I feed my body in order to starve the cancer, the elimination of stress and worry to minimize inflammation in my system, the degree to which I dwell on the goal of what I want versus the prognosis I have been given, and how I reinforce images of disease or health by how I speak and the words I choose. And while these are all worthy vehicles fueling my progress, it's ultimately my driver not the vehicle who holds the keys to my faith, keeps me on course, and delivers me safely to my destination.

I have believed with great confidence that God has both the desire and the ability to heal me according to my faith. It's not been unfounded, wishful thinking. My foundation comes from the many promises of health and healing God gives us in Hebrew and New Testament Scriptures. It's up to me to accept or reject, receive or refuse. Daily, I've searched out, studied, and personalized these promises. I recite them aloud in the first person, present tense to create a fixed, unwavering mind-set. I haven't just hoped it would be God's will to heal me. I believe it is God's will that I am whole as surely as I desire and work to make my son, Nicholas, feel better when he gets sick. And whether God's desire cemented my certainty, or my certainty moved the hand of God, I cannot say. But I do know the night before my PET CT scans, I felt great peace and envisioned Jesus telling me, "Rejoice. Be glad. Stop focusing on yourself. Celebrate. Laugh. My people miss so much of life because they piddle away their time with groaning, worrying, whining, and striving. Rest. Trust. I've got you in the palm of My hand." I actually burst out in uncontrollable laughter with tears and mascara streaking down my face. The more I tried to stop, the more it kept coming over me. I laughed and laughed in utter joy until I was exhausted. It was a weird phenomenon even for me, but I loved every minute of it.

The next morning, I met first with my oncologist who suggested a few clinical trials we might try depending on the outcome of my scans. I smiled politely and responded with all the right words, but in my heart, I knew that none of it would be necessary. She informed me it would take two days before she would get the test results, so we made plans to be in contact with one another by Friday afternoon.

I arrived home that evening and prepared dinner for Brent, Nicholas, and me. Just as we sat down at the table, the phone rang. Typically, we don't answer the phone, but I thought I should check the caller ID in case it was the doctor. It was.

She was amazed that she had already received the reports—just hours from the completion of my scans. She said I must have done something right because that never happens. Then she proceeded to read the findings. She noted some inflammation around the lymph nodes, which was likely to be residual from May's surgery. She also noted some inflammation in the right node of my lung, possibly left over from an undiagnosed case of pneumonia (so that's why I felt so cruddy in June). Then she addressed the metastatic breast cancer lesions on the spine. "There is NO metastatic uptake appearing on the spine." I screamed with excitement and fell to the floor. Brent and Nic were stunned by my reaction, having no idea who was on the other end of the phone. I made her repeat it again and again. "What about the L-2 lesion (lumbar two vertebrae)?" I asked. She replied, "It's not even showing up on the report." "Well, what about the T-12 (where the larger cancer lesion was found)?" She noted the spot is there, but there is no metastatic uptake, meaning, there is no cancerous activity present at this time. She asked if I would still like to consider the clinical trial for some time in the future before she turned her attention to scheduling a six-month re-scan of my body. I agreed politely, knowing full well their intervention would not be necessary.

Healing hugs,
Doreen

Choose "Yes" and "Amen": Celebrating Sustainable Wellness

"For no matter how many promises God has made, they are 'Yes' in Christ. And so through him the 'Amen' is spoken by us to the glory of God" (2 Corinthians 1:20).

My heart and intent for this book is to help you outline areas where you can take hold, take responsibility, and take action so you have confidence to claim healing in the midst of disease or dis-ease. Through *The Spirit to Heal* and *The Mind to Heal*, my prayer is you might come to experience the heart of the Father, the mind of Christ, and the power of the Holy Spirit over every area of your life—body, mind and spirit.

As much as I hope and pray to have an anointing touch to heal every person I pray over, as much as I press God for more power and insight to pour out the healing I have received in my own body over the physical afflictions of others, and as much as I focus on ushering in Jesus' love and compassion into the moment of praying with someone, I must confess there is no formula I've found when it comes to healing. We live in a marketing-driven society that wants to package everything in ten easy steps. I wish with all my heart it were that simple. Even as the chapters of this book detail the active choices we must make to co-create an environment for healing, I am well aware of the limitations of communicating knowledge, insight, and understanding. What's meant to create a living experience often gets reduced to a list of practical principles to live by.

But sustainable wellness is not found in a summary of medical, academic, or spiritual principles. To sustain something is to keep it alive and active, and it must be fed, nurtured, and developed. When it stops growing, it dies. Since the things of this natural world eventually lead to death, our hope and mind-set should be toward the spirit realm, which offers sustainable, eternal life. In other words, maintainable wellness is spirit-driven; it cannot be found in the things of this world. It comes from a regenerated mind controlled by the Spirit, which offers us life and peace.

"Those who live according to the sinful nature have their minds set on what that nature desires; but those who live in accordance with the Spirit have their minds set on what the Spirit desires. The mind of sinful man is death, but the mind controlled by the Spirit is life and peace" (Romans 8:5–6).

When we live according to the natural world, we live by our human instincts and desires. In our finite minds that are bound by time, space, and physical senses, we see and interpret the world from the perspective of "me." Life happens around "me." We match what we see, sense, and experience against our stored subconscious beliefs that define our current reality, our truth, our tangible here-and-now. Because the physical laws of nature apply, we deem "truth" as those things that are verifiable, quantifiable, replicable, rational, and explainable. We pursue the physical and intellectual because we believe if we can define, explain, or manage it, we are in control of it. We even see this occur in spirituality, where religion becomes man's attempt to harness the things of God. When we live exclusively from the natural realm, truth becomes subjective, and we become the center of our own universe where we believe man has dominion and entitlement.

The spirit realm also operates from law, but it operates according to spiritual principles. To the human eye, spiritual reality is unseen and often intangible. Many consider the spirit realm to be elsewhere, another dimension. It's futuristic and is experienced after death. Though theologians and clerics devote their life's pursuit to its study, the things of the spirit realm are cloaked, unexplainable, and miraculous. They cannot be harnessed or controlled. When we live from the spirit realm, God has dominion, and we have inheritance through Christ's shed blood.

For those who hold little regard for the things of the Spirit, they put their stock, their trust, and their hope in what they see and have. They operate under "what you see is what you get." And when they affirm, "I am," the best they can do is dwell in hopeful possibilities.

But even as modern Christians, we too can often find ourselves living primarily from the natural realm. Yes, we believe in the things of the Spirit. We accept the Word of God; we meditate on it, memorize it, and hope in it. We participate in worship, study, missions, ministry, and financial giving, all in efforts to live by those things we hold in conviction to be true. But when dropped into the daily physical circumstances of life, we tend to focus on "truth" as the reality we're experiencing in the natural. In other words, when confronted with challenges, it's our check-ups and checkbooks that become the true measure of what the dominant reality is in our lives.

James 1:23 compares this type of person, one who listens to the Word of God but then doesn't do what it says, to the man who looks at his face in the mirror and then forgets what he looks like the minute he turns away. We get a glimpse or reflection of truth and peace in those quiet times of prayer or Sunday mornings in the pew, but they fade from view as we encounter "real" life throughout the rest of the week.

How do we know if this is the condition of our heart? The evidence is in our self-talk—how we think and speak about our situations. Are you dwelling more on the problem than on the solution? Are you waiting first for external medical evidence to give proof to your internal spiritual inheritance? Are you willing to speak well, saying, "I am healed," before there is any physical evidence that you are? "It is written: I believed, therefore I have spoken" (2

Corinthians 4: 13). Do you have that same spirit of faith to speak it before you see it?

Too often, when our physical situations don't reflect or measure up to what we're praying for, we conclude, "It must not have been God's will." As a result, we don't come to God with a fixed, unwavering mind-set, trusting in His goodness. We don't possess a positive expectation that "without faith it is impossible to please God, because anyone who comes to Him must believe that He exists and that He rewards those who earnestly seek Him" (Hebrews 11:6). We don't actually live from Jesus' proclamation that "Everything is possible for him who believes" (Mark 9:23). Yes, we hope. But healing requires more than hope where "hope" is often "desire without expectancy." The examples of Jesus' healings always contained the element of faith—being certain of what we hope for, desire with expectancy. It's a mind-set of "yes," not "maybe."

Too often, we pray, "If it's your will, God, please heal _____," when Scripture tells us the whole reason Jesus came and died was to conquer death and defeat the ways of the Devil (1 John 3:8). And Jesus won!

"Surely he took up our infirmities and carried our sorrows, yet we considered him stricken by God, smitten by him and afflicted. But he was pierced for our transgressions, he was crushed for our iniquities; the punishment that brought us peace was upon him, and by his wounds we are healed" (Isaiah 53:4–5).

For all generations, Jesus accomplished this victory on the cross. As he was taking his last breath and proclaimed, "*Tetelestai*," he was saying, "It is finished." It is complete. The debt has been paid. There is nothing more Jesus needs to do for us than what He has already done! Our response is not one of grumbling, pleading, and begging. It's "Yes! Amen. Thank you, Jesus, for what You accomplished for me. I trust You and receive *all* You have made available to me." It is reflected in your attitude, the way you speak, the actions you undertake, and your testimony to others. You overcome by the blood of the Lamb and the word of your testimony (Revelation 12:11). You must proclaim it out loud and in deed.

I recall a wonderful little booklet sent to me from my friend's mother when she heard the news of my second cancer diagnosis. It was a brief but powerful story written by Dodi Osteen, mother of the famed Texas preacher, Joel Osteen. Her remarkable story tells of how she was sent home to spend her remaining weeks of life, as doctors were unable to treat her cancer-ridden body. In great pain but with even greater faith, she and her husband meditated on, claimed, recited, and visualized the Word of God and the many Scriptures speaking of God's healing hand and her inheritance to receive.

But what was most liberating, enlightening, and even humorous to me was where Dodi underscores our need to walk the talk of our beliefs. During her illness, she asked for help from her family to move some furniture that was easy enough for an individual to lift. Instead of placating to her fragile medical condition, they insisted she do it herself. At first, she was shocked by the callousness of their response. But in a moment, it became crystal clear. If she truly believed she was healed as she had been speaking from the Scriptures, she needed to demonstrate her faith by acting like she *was* healed. How eye opening! From that moment, she forced herself to go out and serve the needs of others in her congregation. She didn't wait until she was well to think and behave well. She believed, confessed, and acted in accordance with those beliefs, trusting that He, on whose word she stood, is faithful. That was over thirty-five years ago. She has been cancer-free ever since.

Faith is more than memorizing Bible verses. Faith is responsive. It demands action. It's not waiting around to see if something will happen to prove faith has substance. It's picking up one's mat and moving forward when the word is given (Acts 9:32–34). When we continue to pray and plead and beg God for what He's already provided us, it's a form of unbelief and rejection. We dismiss the goodness of God toward us and push away the benefits and blessings of the cross over our lives in place of the visible circumstances we face. That's why the apostle Paul emphasizes in 2 Corinthians 4:18, "We [should] fix our eyes not on what is seen, but on what is unseen. For what is seen is temporary, but what is unseen is eternal."

When I attended a healing service the night before my PET CT scans, I felt this truth to be so evident in my heart. As a result, I was momentarily conflicted when the prayer team came and asked how they could pray for me. I had to tell them I was not asking specifically for healing because to have them repeat and pray for something I believed I had already received would do one of two things: 1) give evidence to a lack of faith in already appropriating God's promises for me; or 2) have their prayers be of no real value since they would be praying for something I already had. What I did ask for was prayer that my mind would catch up with my spirit of faith so I would not be plagued with moments of doubt or entertain "what if" with every ache and pain my body tried to communicate. What happened next was a supernatural encounter (see *The Spirit to Heal*), which gave me the sustaining power to be free from doubt. God showed me that faith does not grow and healing does not occur from acting on a list of spiritual principles; they come from abiding in the place of His intimate presence.

Structured by Principles, Transformed by Presence

When we live from the natural realm, we live in the *midst* of our circumstances; when we live from the spirit realm, we live *above* our circumstances. When we live from the natural realm, our eyes are fixed on the *problem*; when we live from the spirit realm, our eyes envision the *solution*. When we live from the natural realm, we focus on our *need for healing*; when we live from the spirit realm, we gaze on the face of the *Healer*. When we live from the natural realm, the best we can do is live by heavenly *principles*; when we live from the spirit realm, we abide in the heavenly *Presence*.

Too often, too many of us are trying to manage and live our lives by godly principles. "Just give me the steps, and tell me how to do it!!!" And for some, like me, our personalities or temperaments are more readily geared that way. We are principle-centered people. We seek justice; we pursue excellence; we love learning; we rally for truth. While this looks good on the outside, the shortfall with principle-centered living is it can often be void of love, peace, and power on the inside. When we build our lives around godly principles alone, we can too easily become performance-driven and perfectionistic and wind up missing the power of God's presence. When we build our expectations on principle-centered living, we run the risk of being disappointed, envious, bitter, comparative, vengeful, and withholding when there are no more hoops to jump through. The outcomes don't seem to live up to our methodologies. And we find ourselves at the end of ourselves, having expended lots of energy upholding lots of rules but finding ourselves still short of the goal.

Principle-centered living often sits on the sidelines of faithfulness where we look the part of a devoted fan without really experiencing the thrill of the game. We're so busy analyzing the plays and developing strategy that we disengage from the intimate power and passion of the players. It's the difference between living from your head and connecting with your heart. Principles order the mind; presence feeds the spirit. Principles are helpful and healthy as they clarify parameters, provide structure, and communicate direction. But principles without the presence of God lack the power to heal. When God is present, He permeates and changes the environment from sickness to health, sin to forgiveness, and strife to peace. He has to. He is the Spirit of all love and life. His transforming presence is the effect of spiritual law.

God always seeks to save and redeem. It's His nature; it's His character. He's a rewarder of those who believe in His goodness and approach Him with the confident, unquestioning trust of a child. "Why?" is tempered by the quiet spirit of faith in who He is and the testimony of what He's done throughout history.

The mysteries of God cannot explain why He acts in our lives as He does. While we can be sure His nature is good, faithful, trustworthy, and steadfast, His purposes often remain veiled. At times, God breaks into our reality with what I call the "descending hand of God." He can heal anyone of any demeanor at any time in an instantaneous way we refer to as "a miracle." It is our human conditioning and response to continuously press God for those miraculous moments in our most dire straits.

But the journey where God desires to draw us up higher into His presence to live in and from the realities of heaven is just as supernatural. This "ascending hand of God" extends to us in open invitation as He responds to our cries, "Yes. I have accomplished this for you. Join Me. Trust Me. Live in the light of My presence. It is yours to abide in. Take My hand, and see what I will do."

The problem most of us encounter is, we are conditioned from birth to seek permission. We live in the reluctance and hesitancy of, "Oh, may I have _____? Thank you!" in most areas of our lives. We have learned to seek permission and advancement from parents, teachers, coaches, clergy, professors, employers, and the like. As a result, we live under the scrutiny of "am I good enough, worthy enough, faithful enough, smart enough, or purposeful enough" to be promoted?

When we live from this subconscious conditioned mind-set, we don't live from inheritance; we live from insecurity. We don't dwell in authority; we dwell in apprehension. We don't exercise power; we excuse unclaimed possession. We keep asking for help and waiting, begging for change and wondering, and all the while Christ is saying, "*Yes* … step up." We keep focusing on the problem and pleading, and Jesus says, "Yes … I'm here." We define ourselves by the realities of the natural realm, and Christ says, "Define yourselves according to the glorious riches you have in me (Philippians 4:19). Define yourselves by the realities of the kingdom of heaven. Live on Earth … as it *is* in heaven,"(Matthew 6:10).

When you abide in Christ and Christ abides in you, a *Holy Transfusion* occurs. Most of us, as followers of Jesus, are hooked up to the "blood transfusion machine"—we have connected ourselves to Christ—but we never receive the flow of new blood because we don't turn it on. We keep waiting for permission! We are saved to eternity, but we remain spiritually, physically, and emotionally anemic on Earth and don't access the lifeline of abundant living. Let this take root in your spirit: *Your potential in Christ Jesus IS your permission to step up into supernatural inheritance. You don't have to keep asking. You need to start proclaiming "Yes" and "Amen."* This is not just a theological position or intellectual assumption. You and I hold God's redemptive glory in the very molecules of our bodies.

Jesus' fingerprint of power is pervasive and interdependent in everything He has created. He doesn't limit or compartmentalize His glory and our access into certain places and not others. We do that through the limitations of our own understanding. We separate God's truth and categorize His promises according to what's spiritual or secular, present or eternal, anticipated or miraculous. But God's handiwork is always available and multidimensional. When He wrote history, He proclaimed it to the prophets but also declared it up in the stars, down in the sea, and within the formation of all living things. He left nothing untouched. He even went so far as to genetically imprint the power of the cross into our very DNA.

In the cells and tissues of nearly every living organism, scientists have found a glycoprotein network called laminin. This structure is foundational for life because it is responsible for tissue survival and cell adhesion. In other words, laminin is what holds us together at the cellular level. Laminins are also called trimeric proteins because they are triune in nature—a characteristic of being made in the image of our triune God—containing an α-chain, a β-chain, and a γ-chain. When viewed by scientists under electron microscopy, these three protein chains intertwine to form the shape of a cross! God has deposited His signature into all He has created. He placed the healing power of the cross not only in our spirits but in our bodies as well. Colossians 1:15–17 tells us,

> He [Jesus] is the image of the invisible God, the firstborn over all creation. For by him all things were created: things in heaven and on earth, visible and invisible, whether thrones or power or rulers or authorities; all things were created by him and for him. He is before all things, *and in him all things hold together* (emphasis mine).

His restoring power within us is only limited by our hearts and minds. As we dwell in the enormity of His brilliance, marvel at the intensity of His love for us, and respond to these truths within us, their transforming effect begins to invade our heart, soul, and body.

Abundance in Life Cycle

When we begin to yearn more for the heart of the Healer than we do the healing, and when we quiet the reasoning mind and connect our spirit to the Spirit of love and life, we begin to experience the ascending hand of Jesus Christ who sets us free and opens the way to the spirit realm for us.

As we posture ourselves more and more in God's *Presence*, we begin to reflect more and more of His character. His presence imparts His divine nature over our body, mind, and spirit, giving us everything we need for life and godliness (2 Peter 3). His presence opens up to us the transforming influence of His *Perspective* (Romans 12:2). Holy Perspective reveals and authorizes God's *Permission* for us to access His death-defying *Power*—the same Holy Spirit that raised Christ from the dead and is now in us (Romans 8:11). God enables this so we, His ambassadors, can take *Possession* of the territory satan has tried to steal and destroy from us. This territory is the physical, emotional, and spiritual experience of abundant life. Our empowerment and gifting from the Holy Spirit equips us to fight aggressively and victoriously for that which satan has corrupted. As we reclaim our inheritance, we expand our *Position* of authority and influence in Christ. This restoration releases us to live from a deeper truth in our identity and operate in a higher level of *Potential*.

In this encounter with the heavenly, we become more than moral, faithful followers trying to maintain a stiff upper lip through the hardships of life. We are even "more than conquerors," (Romans 8:37) shoring up resources of confidence and courage for the next battle. Our engagement is more than cyclical in nature. It is ascending, taking us into higher realms of possibility.

As we cultivate the relationship of Divine Presence that transforms our Perspective and reveals God's Permission to access His Power so we can reclaim Possession and apprehend greater Position to live from limitless Potential, we experience expanding opportunity. In other words, our victories in God become our memorials and testaments to take on bigger challenges with even greater reliance. We grow upward and outward from glory to glory. It's not about how strong we are in faith but about how strong God's power is in our lives. The promises are already "Yes." It's the response of the transformed spirit, mind, and body in alignment and with positive expectation to celebrate the "Amen!" in Christ Jesus.

It is in this worshipful, patient, trusting, and enduring relationship of Presence with God where we see His intentions for accessing abundant life in the "land of the living." It is His to offer; it is ours to choose.

> Now what I am commanding you today is not too difficult for you or beyond your reach. It is not up in heaven, so that you have to ask, "Who will ascend into heaven to get it and proclaim it to us so we may obey it?" Nor is it beyond the sea, so that you have to ask, "Who will cross the sea to get it and proclaim it to us so we may obey it?" No, the word

is very near you; it is in your mouth and in your heart so you may obey it.

See, I set before you today life and prosperity, death and destruction. For I command you today to love the Lord your God, to walk in his ways, and to keep his commands, decrees, and laws; then you will live and increase and the Lord your God will bless you in the land you are entering to possess (Deuteronomy 30:11--17).

Picture Perfect:
Creating Health and Wellness in the Midst of Disease

Blog Entry: October, 2009

Afterglow

THE PAST FEW WEEKS HAVE been amazing for me, not as much for what God has done in my body, but for how it is impacting the people around me. Don't get me wrong ... I absolutely hold a deep awe and gratitude for what God has allowed me to walk through in this entire experience! It's profoundly humbling. But "amazed" to me offers an element of surprise that just wasn't there before. For as surely as I know that when I sit down a chair will support me, I have been confident that what God says He will do, He will do.

The reaction of others, on the other hand, has stunned me. Nothing has been more celebratory than sharing the news of my recent PET CT scans with family, friends, and colleagues. Among the throngs of well-wishers, I've been most impressed by the similarity of genuine expressions such as, "I heard (or read) your news, and it brought tears to my eyes," or "I actually got goosebumps when I found out the news."

Some of the more intriguing comments have been around the validity of the tests, both current as well as the original diagnoses. "Are you sure you got the right results back?" "Are you positive you were properly diagnosed in the first place?" Even amongst family I've had to recount the litany of tests, including an MRI, PET CT scans, a lumbar MRI, and bone biopsy performed among three different institutions and confirmed by two different labs: stage four breast cancer metastasized to the spine.

It's been quite a revelation to see that what we hope for and what we expect are not always one and the same. You see it in the shock, suspicion, and surprise of reactions—particularly from those who earnestly prayed for healing. Hope is important. Hope allows us to dream and want. It's a goal-setter. But hope alone holds no substance. We can hope for something but never take any affirmative action toward it. Hope gives us the picture, but faith is what causes us to step out.

In other words, what we pray for in one moment and what we go on to say to ourselves and others about our situation can be two different things. You see it evidenced in the way people respond to the circumstances, challenges, or outcomes in their lives. It shows up when we truly hope and pray for a positive resolution but find ourselves shocked, amazed, or suspicious when it actually manifests. It's as if we wear a cloak of caution so as not to become too exposed in case the results don't match our desires. We label ourselves as a "realist," a "pragmatist," a practical person who prefers to stay grounded in what he or she knows and knows how to cause. But if we honestly examine the space between what we want and what we actually expect, we'll often find ourselves trapped in a land of limiting beliefs: "There's no real cure for stage four cancer"; "Alternative interventions, herbs, and supplements don't work"; "What you eat doesn't matter. It's all in your genetics"; "God doesn't perform healing miracles today"; and "What if it's not God's will or desire to heal?"

Subconsciously, we wind up creating our own self-fulfilling prophecies and subverting healing as our doubts become more dominant than our dreams.

Healing hugs,
Doreen

Personal Affirmations for Life and Wholeness:

I keep the Word of God before my eyes and sealed in my heart because it has transforming truth and the power to heal.

I am the body of Christ, and cancer has no power over me, for He who is in me (the spirit of God) is greater than the things of this world.

I am positive and peaceful about my health. I feed my body with the good results I expect.

Cancer, you must go! Deadly destructive cells, you must leave! My body belongs to Christ and is a temple of the Holy Spirit.

I have been purchased with a great price. I am God's, and He is mine. His life and Spirit pulsate through my body.

Because I am a child of God, sickness, fear, and oppression have no power over me.

My immune system is strong and healthy. My natural killer cells (NKs) effectively slaughter micro-cancer cells throughout my body.

I command my blood cells to cut off, destroy, and eliminate every rogue cancer cell that tries to inhabit my body. I command every cell of my body to be normal in Jesus' name.

Praise the Lord, oh my soul, and *all* that is within me comes into submission to praise God's holy name.

Rivers of living water wash over every cell from the top of my head to the tip of my toes, cleansing and renewing life and wholeness in me.

I thank God I am fearfully and wonderfully made. I affirm my body and give thanks that I am His.

I intentionalize my thoughts toward health, peace, and positive expectations.

Every cell that does not promote life and health in my body is expelled. My vigilant immune system will not allow tumors to thrive in my body.

I am an overcomer. My body responds to the direction I give it.

My mind and body awaken each morning feeling strong, refreshed, and vibrant for the day.

The same Spirit that raised Jesus from the dead dwells in me, permeating His life through my veins and sending healing throughout my body.

Cancer is so limited. It cannot cripple love; it cannot shatter hope; it cannot erode faith; it cannot eat away peace; it cannot destroy confidence; it cannot kill friendship; it cannot shut out memories; it cannot silence courage; it cannot invade the soul; it cannot reduce eternal life; it cannot quench the Spirit; it cannot lessen the power of the resurrection.

—Author Unknown

ABOUT THE AUTHOR

DOREEN LECHELER IS A PERSONAL development expert, two-time cancer conqueror and coach, author, and engaging speaker.

With a passion and purpose to unleash the God-given excellence in others, Doreen teaches steps to create constructive, successful, high performing outcomes. Whether she's been working with leaders of a nation, a community, an organization, or individuals battling chronic disease, Doreen stresses the critical nature of learning how to manage our minds.

She began a professional career in the non-profit sector after a seven-year tenure of international fashion modeling. Doreen excelled to senior leadership positions in both national and international non-profit organizations. Using her business and marketing acumen, she was responsible for overseeing growth in program development, business development, and organizational advancement.

In 2000, she combined her background in business, human behavior, and cognitive psychology to begin building peak performance, leadership development, employee engagement, and change management in a variety of organizations across the U.S., including finance, telecommunications, non-profit, faith-based, sales and marketing, customer service, manufacturing, social services, government, education, transportation, and health care.

Along with her dedication to see people grow in meaningful and measurable ways, Doreen is devoted to helping individuals develop a faith-filled mindset toward healing. As a two-time cancer conqueror, Doreen speaks extensively on her journey and the spirit-mind-body strategy that fostered her own healing of "incurable" stage four cancer with metastases to the bone.

She is the author of two books. *The Spirit to Heal* is Doreen's personal cancer story of the power of faith for healing. It stresses the importance of *what* to think in the midst of disease. *The Mind to Heal* emphasizes our role and responsibility to receive healing. It outlines life-giving steps for *how* to think in the midst of disease. Doreen is also the creator and facilitator of the self-paced, personal development program, *Destiny Living: Unleashing the Heart of Your Purpose-Filled Potential.*

Are you ready to make your destiny a reality?
Do you just need an extra push?
Want to find solutions to take your life to the next level?
Visit www.TheMindToHeal.com/offer for
an exciting opportunity
and exclusive offer for readers only, and get started TODAY!

For more information on Doreen Lecheler's
programs, speaking engagements, materials, and books,
contact: www.DoreenLecheler.com
office@visionlinked.com